THE ULTIMATE *You*

ACHIEVING GREATNESS

CURTIS KESSINGER

Copyright © 2012 Curtis Kessinger

All rights reserved. No part of this book may be reproduced or transmitted in any form or by any means without the written permission of the publisher, except in the case of brief excerpts embodied in published articles and reviews.

The author has taken precaution in the development of this material and believes it to be accurate, however, neither the author nor publisher assumes any responsibility for any errors or omissions. The author and publisher are not liable for use of this material by any individual as their interpretation and results may vary.

Published by Blue Heron Publications

Interior formatting and cover design
by Kimberly Martin of Jera Publishing

Kessinger, Curtis
The Ultimate You!

Paperback Book
ISBN-10: 0-9777279-2-0
ISBN 13: 978-0-9777279-2-6

Acknowledgments

This book is dedicated to my parents and siblings for allowing me to develop into an independent, go-for-it type of person; to my wife Jan and kids for continuing to support my endeavors and showing me what is most important in life; and to my friends for the great ride we have been on and continue to be on.

Special thanks go out to my wife, and friends Brett Figueroa and Rhonda Moskowitz, for their help in writing this book. Without them it would not have happened. If you ever run across their path, thank them dearly.

This book is also dedicated to those out there willing to go after their dreams until they take their last breath. Everything you need to achieve greatness is inside of you. Nothing can stop you on your journey. It is only a matter of time before you are The Ultimate You.

Contents

Introduction 1

Success Mindset 9

    Purpose.. 10
    Freedom 11
    Happiness.. 12
    Yesterday Was a Long Time Ago 13
    Dream It, Believe It, and Achieve It! 17
    The Zone.. 22
    Retrain... 25
    Motivation 29
    Attitude 30
    The Right Thing 31
    Decision and Change 32
    Planting Seeds 33
    Success Thoughts 34
    Learning 37
    Rejection 38
    Deal With It - Rejection 39
    Separation 40
    Failure Is Great 41
    Pain.. 43
    Commitment 44
    Focus 45
    Discipline 47
    No Excuses 47
    Living a Great Life.. 47
    Conclusion.. 48

Success Management 49

    Managing Time 49
    Procrastination... 51
    Overcoming Procrastination.. 53
    Balance 54
    Habits 54
    Step-By-Step 55
    Creating Your Future - Goal Setting................................ 56
    Be An Action Hero 62
    Managing Lean.. 64
    Stress Kills - Managing Stress 64

Dealing With Stress 65
Managing Your Environment 67
Leverage With Assistants And Outsourcing 68
Leadership – Managing People 69
Managing Your Database... 70
Managing Your Finances 71
Conclusion.. 73

Success Marketing 75

Product Life Cycle 76
Marketing Plan... 77
The Test Market 85
Press 85
Cross-Platform Marketing 87
Traditional Media 87
The Internet 87
Mobile Media 87
Audio/Video 88
Writing Advertisement Copy 89
People.. 91
Perception 92
Body Language.. 92
What People Demand 93
Negotiation.. 93
Schmoozing/Networking 95
Say What 97
Schmoozing Musts 99
Where To Schmooze 101
Cold Calling... 102
Words of Influence.. 104
Referrals 105
Professional Partnering 105
Joint Ventures.. 106
Affiliates/Independent Salespeople 106
Conclusion... 106

About the Author 109

Appendix 111

Daily Log 112
Biography Sheet 115

Introduction

*"It is your life! You, and only you,
can make it what you want!"*

Welcome to the rest of your life! Are you ready for big things to happen? I know your dreams are sitting up there inside of your head and turning your dreams into reality is very simple if you follow the basics of success in everything you do. You do not want your dreams to go unfulfilled like they do for most people. You are fully capable of achieving success in every area of your life if you are willing to do it. That is the ultimate truth.

Your future is yours to create. It is all up to you. Your imagination determines where you go. If you can imagine it, then you can accomplish it. Nothing is more powerful than an idea and every idea starts in your mind. Most people do not create their future, because they have no idea what they want. Even when they do figure it out, they fail to take action to go after it. Instead of acting on what they want, they go through life reacting to what happens to them. They do what everyone else does and they get what everyone else gets. Success is inside of you and now is the time to get it out. It is time to get busy. That red stoplight that your life has been sitting at has now turned green. It is time to start living the life you want to live.

Imagine for one moment that you are at the end of your life and looking back. Will you have done everything you dreamed of doing? Will you have lived the life you imagined? Will you have improved the lives of others?

Are you happy with where you are in your life? There is no reason for you to settle for a life that you do not want. You must look at all areas of your life, because everything is connected. Your personal life impacts your professional life and visa versa. What areas of your life would you like to change? If things need to change then they need to change, and only you can change them. It is your choice. You get to choose whatever you want. What kind of education, career, home, car, family, friends, vacations, heath, wealth, happiness, giving/volunteering, spirituality, etc., do you want? You can choose to do something, or choose to do nothing. Doing nothing is a choice. Most people choose to do nothing. If you choose to do nothing then you know what to expect for the rest of your life. You can choose to earn more income or not. Choose to have better relationships or not. Choose to learn more or not. Choose to give back and help others or not. Choose to achieve as much as you can or not. Most people make choices that slowly close them off from living a successful life. As they age, their life circle gets smaller and smaller until they are finally watching their dreams and life pass them by, with nothing to keep them going. It is up to you to make the choice to live a successful life. Your success shows what choices you make.

What is your definition of success? Is it the job of your dreams? Is it to own your own business? Is it having a great family? Is it living in a multi-million dollar beach house? Is it living in a tent in the woods? Is it to reach spiritual enlightenment? Is it to open up a homeless shelter? Is it ten billion dollars? What is it for you? How do you measure success? Most people focus on the accumulation of wealth as their measuring stick of success. You can have all the money and material things you want and still not be happy. Happiness is the key ingredient to success, and happiness comes from inside of you. It is an internal feeling that you cannot buy with all the riches in the world. Everything depends on what you want out of your life.

My reason for writing this book is to give you what I have discovered while studying successful people over the last ten years. In here you will find what you need to be successful, allowing you to accomplish everything you want in your life, including obtaining wealth. The ultimate level of success you should be striving to reach is greatness, because greatness leads to happiness. Greatness is not based upon you making the most money, living in the largest estate, driving the most expensive cars, vacationing at the most luxurious destinations, etc. Greatness means doing everything the right way and helping others. Helping others means you do not expect anything in return for your help. No financial gain, press release or thank-you, nothing but the feeling you get inside when you give to someone else. Everything you do impacts others in some way and the only thing I want from you is that your impact is positive. The great basketball coaching legend John Wooden said, "You cannot live a perfect day until you do something for someone who will never be able to repay you." Greatness comes from how you impact the world while you are here and how your impact carries on long after you are gone. Live life to the fullest and inspire others to do the same. You must look for the best in people. Anyone meeting you should leave the meeting better than when he or she arrived. That is greatness. I dare you to be great!

Most people do not realize how simple it is to turn their life around. First, you have to decide to do it. You, and only you, are responsible for what happens. You can accomplish whatever success you want, but will you? Most people will not. They are capable, but most people expect things to change and improve without them doing anything differently than what they are currently doing. In order to change your life you must overcome that part of you that does not want to change. Decide right now to change and you can have whatever success you can imagine. Today is a different day. You have never been through this day before in your life. Whatever you want to happen today can happen, but it is up to you.

Let us make one thing perfectly clear. Everyone is looking for the secret to success, but there is no secret. There is no secret path, no secret formula, no magic bullet, and no magic dust to sprinkle over the top of you. **The only secret is that there is no secret.** That might sound like bad news to you, but the good news is that it does not take superhuman ability to be successful. Success is not reserved for certain people based on their talent or education, their looks, their wealth, etc. It does not matter if you are 16 years old or 116 years old. It does not matter if you failed in the past or were unsuccessful your entire life. What matters is learning and using the simple basics of success, which you will learn in this book.

Most people are not as successful as they want because they cannot control themselves. They cannot resist all of the temptations that ruin their financial security, their relationships, their physical health, etc. They cannot self regulate their own behavior. It all starts within the mind and ends with their daily behavior. It all has to be controlled.

Successful people stand apart from everyone else because they do not do what everyone else does. They do not follow the masses of people nor look for approval from them. They do not sit back and wait for someone else to help them. They take charge of their life. They are able to control their mind and their actions on a daily basis. They take action. They know there is always a way to make things happen, a way to get things done. Their motto is never to give up, because they know there is no future in giving up. They do not blame others or make up excuses. They know the results they get do not depend entirely on hard work. There are many unsuccessful hard workers. They know it takes hard work, but they know they must work smarter, not necessarily harder. Successful people always take a step, no matter how small, because it moves them forward.

Your past is important, because it is the main reason you are where you are right now. Everything that has happened in your life up to this point is your back-story, your history. You must take a brief look at your history and then move forward. No more looking back wishing things might have turned out differently. From now on things are going to be much different. Start today on your road to success. Everyone falls into the trap of thinking tomorrow is going to be a better day. They wish away today and wait for tomorrow to arrive. They think they will be happy once this happens, or that happens, or once they get this, or get that. No more waiting for tomorrow, because it is not coming. Today is the day!

The Book

This book was designed to provide you with the principles/tools to create whatever success you want and allow you to get past any temporary setbacks that are guaranteed to show up. You will find different strategies, some you will agree with and some you might not. Some material is repeated in this book, because repetition is the only way to learn a new language and success has its own language. This book is broken up into three main parts: Mindset, Management and Marketing. These parts are then expanded into various topics. Mindset, Management, and Marketing cover the three main areas you must master to be successful. Mindset starts with you, and what is inside of your head, then Management goes the next step to cover your daily life and Marketing goes the last step to cover the world in which you must operate to be successful.

Mindset. What matters most is having the right mindset to be successful. Your mind is the biggest obstacle standing in your way. You might think there are other obstacles preventing you from achieving huge success, but they are only symptoms of the real problem, and the real problem is inside your head. You might think everything is okay, but it is not okay if things are not right in your life. When you look inside your mind, you will find that your mind is your main obstacle to your success.

Management. So you never wanted to be in management? Well, you are now! You are in charge of one person and that person is **YOU**! It is a seven-day-a-week job! No snow days, sick days, vacation days, or weekends off when it comes to managing yourself. You have to manage your life. You have to plan it. For some unknown reason most people do not plan their daily life. They plan their vacation, but not the other days of the year. What would your vacation be like if you did not plan it? What if you just jumped inside of your car and started driving without knowing where you were going or why? Your vacation would be a mess. Most people make a mess of their life, because they have no idea where they are going or why. Imagine a student going to class and the instructor has no lesson planned or a worker going to work where they have no work planned. Everyone would waste most of the day trying to figure out what to do. How long would that instructor be employed? How long would that company be in business? Not long at all. You must figure out your life in advance of each day, so that you live each day to the fullest.

Marketing. Marketing? Why marketing? It is all marketing! Marketing covers every aspect of your life. Everything you see involves marketing. Everything you buy involves marketing. Everywhere you go involves marketing. Every job you try to get involves marketing. Your success in life depends on marketing. So, remember one thing about marketing. It is all marketing!

I use the word goal in this book to represent whatever it is that you dream of achieving in your life. Some people hate the word goal so feel free to use whatever word you want to use. What matters is that you pursue the life that you want. If you were wishing for a second chance and a new start in life, then today is the day it starts.

Welcome to your first assignment. Assignments? More schoolwork? You thought school was over? It is never over. Chalk this up as education, not school. It is time to look at the **Daily Log** (in the Appendix). Make up your own log on a piece of paper or on a computer, etc. Use the log as an example for keeping track of everything you do for the next 7 days, and I mean **everything**. Write it down! If you blow your nose, write it down and write it down immediately after it happens. If you wait until the end of the day to record what you did all day you will forget most of it. Also write down the emotions you feel while going about the tasks of your day. Become very aware of how you spend your time and how you feel during that time. How do you start your day? Do you start with a shower, eating breakfast, gym workout, watching TV, reading the newspaper or surfing the internet? Do you get up early or late? Do you hit the snooze alarm ten times before crawling out of bed? You have a routine, but is it a great routine or a bad routine? Does it push you closer to achieving the success you want, or does it push you further away? Take notice and write it down. Write down every phone call, every meal, every time you walk to the refrigerator and peek inside, every time you look out the window, every time you click on your email or surf the internet, etc.

Every single minute counts. You must be like an accountant, but instead of determining where every penny went, you must determine where every minute went. You will be shocked when you find out how much time you waste every day of the week. You must be aware of where your time goes. Pay attention or pay the price.

Welcome to the rest of your life!

Curtis Kessinger

1
Success Mindset

"What would you do if you believed you could do anything?"

Welcome to the Mindset Material. Successful people know that the main difference between them and everyone else is their mindset. You have to have the right mindset to be successful. Your mind can both help you and hurt you. It can be your best friend and your worst enemy. Your brain is just the physical part of your body, but your mind is made up of all the beliefs that lead to your behavior and actions. Your mind controls everything you do. Your brain is the storage unit and your mind is everything stored in there. You are simply going to clean it out and replace that old stuff with better and newer stuff. Your mind is the most powerful part of your body so you have to keep it active and in shape. Use your mind or it uses you.

Successful people have the belief that they will succeed. Even as they struggle they continue to believe in success. They keep their mind open, which allows them to see opportunities that others with a closed mind do not see. They do not see problems as problems. They see problems as opportunities. They are always ready to make the decisions they need to make. They do not have to **get** ready, because they **are** ready. Most people believe that no matter what they do they will not be successful. If that is your belief then you will not succeed. That is a guarantee. You have to turn your beliefs and actions into the beliefs and actions of the most successful people on the face of this earth. You do not have to make major life changes. The changes are simple.

Your current mindset has gotten you to where you are and if you do not like where you are then you have to change and create a new mindset. If you change your mind you change your life. If you cannot change then you will continue to get what you have been getting. Making slight changes to your mindset makes a huge difference in everything you do. The people around you will start to notice that something is different about you. You will act differently, you will look differently, and you may even walk differently. Everything about you will be different.

You need to improve every single day. Each step you take has to be a step forward, not sideways or backwards. Some days you will feel like you have made progress and other days you will feel like you have lost ground. If you learn something from those bad days then it is still progress. You must be willing to take a few lumps. You are going to get knocked down, but what matters is how long you stay down. Most people never get back up. They get knocked down once and stay down for the rest of their life and they use it as an excuse to stay down. You must get back up and come back stronger, smarter and more determined than ever before.

You are a remarkable person and capable of doing remarkable things. No one on the face of this earth is like you. No one sees, feels, thinks, chooses, acts, etc., the way you do. You bring things to the world that no one else can bring. You have gifts. Everything you need is already inside of your head and your heart. It is simply a matter of pulling it out and putting it to good use. You get out of life whatever you put into it. If you put little in, you get little out. If you put a lot in, you get a lot out.

Purpose

What is your purpose? Do you know? Purpose means living every minute, going after what you are supposed to be going after, in all areas of your life. Knowing your purpose is key to your success. You have to know your who, what, when, where and why of your life. Who are you, and who do you want to become? What do you want? When do you want it? Where do you want to live, work, travel, etc.? Why are you the way you are? Why do you want whatever you want? Chasing after the wrong things never makes you happy, and you will never achieve success. It drains the life out of you. Get excited about what you are doing. You have to have good reasons for spending your time the way you do. Your motivation must come from within. If you cannot determine your main purpose in life then you will always be wondering and struggling. You will work at a job you will not like. You will buy things thinking they will provide you with what you want. You will get into relationships that are doomed from the start. You can feel it if what you are doing is right. Are you chasing after the right things? Even if you obtain the most wealth on the planet, will it fulfill you? If you obtain it by pursuing what you truly want, then that is worth doing. Therefore, you must figure it out. When you figure it out you will use it in every decision you make. What is it that you have a natural energy to do? What is it that you love to do, that you might be able to do to earn your income? Saturate your thoughts with what you want and find a way to get it.

Write down what you want and place it where you will see it daily. Your mind will automatically assist you in developing step-by-step plans and taking action to get it. To reach your potential you have to be able to imagine it first. You need desire to achieve something. Achieving long-term success requires long-term desire. As soon as you determine your purpose, only then can your mind begin to work on achieving it.

Freedom

A huge part of being successful is reaching a point of total freedom. Most people have not experienced it. What is it that will give you freedom? Freedom is a feeling of being able to do what you want, with whom you want, when you want, without fear. Imagine waking up every day looking forward to what you are going to do that day. You would be in complete control of your life. Having a free and open mind is the first step to total freedom.

Happiness

True happiness is not an occasional feeling you have, but a feeling you have the majority of the time. Why is happiness so hard for most people to obtain? The reason is that they are looking in the wrong place. They are looking outside of themselves. It comes from inside, not outside. You cannot buy your way to happiness. It is not something you own. The happiest people in the world often have the least amount of wealth. The general thought is that by having more of something happiness will arrive and life will be great. Sure, it would be nice to own the things of your dreams, but it will not be enough to make you happy. Ask yourself why so many wealthy people are not happy? Do not mistake pleasure for happiness. Pleasure is temporary. It gives you the sensation of happiness, but it wears off very quickly. Pleasure can become an addiction. That is why you cannot pursue happiness by things outside of you. You want the permanent feeling of happiness and that comes from within you, and your mind is the key. It is up to you to determine your definition of happiness.

The single most important key to being happy is being the person you are meant to be. You cannot be happy being someone else or being the person that everyone else wants you to be. Usually what you want and what you need are two completely different things. Your wants are often the shiny material things that do not satisfy internal needs. You see what someone else has and you want it too. Every advertisement is selling you what they say you need to be happy. Advertisers know that most people buy products based on emotions, not logic. The advertisement shows you the dream life you can have if you own those products. But, someone always has a bigger boat, nicer car, finer jewelry, more lavish house, etc. If you love movies, the great characters you root for are the ones who get what they need, not necessarily what they want. They get the love, respect, integrity and security that they need, but they may not get wealthy. I want you to get everything you want, but the internal needs are at the top of the list. Get those and you can be happy.

Happiness does not mean you are only happy when things are going right. When things are not going right you should be happy to take on the challenge. You should like the challenge. You should like being in the game of life rather than watching from the sidelines. You should be able to handle the things that are thrown at you on a daily basis.

Your spirituality and/or religion may be a big part of your happiness. I want you to believe whatever you want to believe. It is no one else's business to tell you what to believe. What is right for you may not be right for anyone else.

True happiness comes from the feelings you have inside of you. So how do you focus on the inner results as well as the outer results? How do you work on you? You have to determine what you are meant to do. Are you only seeking happiness for you or for others as well? You have to determine what gives you the most satisfaction in your life. Remember, it is a fulfilling feeling, not a thing. When you have that feeling, then you have achieved true happiness.

Yesterday Was a Long Time Ago

You have often heard that history repeats itself and for most people it is true. Their future is built on the foundation made up of their past. Their past controls everything they do for the rest of their life unless they are ready to analyze their past and make changes. Your past influenced who you are, but that has nothing to do with who you can become. It is time to find out who you are by taking one step back into your past. Once you review your past then it is time to move on, because living in the past is not living.

Everyone travels with baggage. It is like carrying extra weight around all day long. It slows you down and prevents you from being your best. Some people carry their baggage better than others. Some have a small bag that weighs them down as if it weighed two tons and others have a huge bag that does not weigh them down at all. It is almost impossible to eliminate all your baggage. It is always present, like those old suitcases handed down generation to generation. To say that you can simply snap your fingers and your past will disappear is just not realistic. Running away and trying to hide from your past is not the answer either, because the past runs and hides with you. Face up to the facts. Trying to deal with critical issues on your own may not always be in your best interest. Do not be afraid to seek outside professional help if you need it. You do not want your baggage to act as a roadblock and limit your progress.

The only way to truly grow and follow your own path is to know yourself. You cannot change anything if you are not aware of it in the first place. It is like taking your car to a mechanic. They have to figure out the problem and where is it coming from. To fix yourself you need to know what needs fixing and what is causing it before you can fix it. Only then, can you become the true you. Once you know who you are, you can determine if you really like who you are. If you do not like who you are then it is time to change.

You experience and perceive things differently than everyone else. You have your own sense of reality. In order for you to overcome everything in your way, you need to be able to understand how you view reality. For example, we have all known someone who was, or is dating the wrong person for them. Everyone else can see it, but not them. They do not see it because they have a distorted view. Their emotions are hiding the reality that this person is not right for them. It is almost impossible for people to see their own flaws. Too many people think things are fine when they are not, and this causes them to delay making changes to correct their life.

Since people are creatures of habit they tend to do things a certain way, because they were always done that way. You have developed habits of thinking that were most likely developed by copying someone else or listening to what someone else said. Most of these habits were formed long before you were old enough to think for yourself. You were taught to do things a certain way so you automatically thought you were doing things right. Your beliefs were influenced from day one by your family, teachers, friends, strangers, society, television, internet, religion, news, authority, etc., and those beliefs may continue to shape you depending on how deeply you believe and adhere to those beliefs.

Group dynamics are especially influencing. For the most part, you want to connect with people and fit in, so you wear the same clothes, fix your hair the same way, say and do the things you know people say and do, etc. It is more comfortable being in a group than standing alone. Staying in a group limits your experience and tolerance of others that do not fit within that group. Often times, you do not follow that little voice inside your head telling **you to be you**. It is extremely hard to go off on your own and not give in to group pressure. All of these influences have helped to develop your mind for both the good and the bad.

The brain is like any muscle, the more you use it the stronger it becomes. The more you focus on a certain belief the stronger that belief becomes. The more you learn about something, the more experienced you become. If a parent, teacher or friend constantly bombards you with a belief, then that belief becomes stronger, no matter whether the belief is good or bad for you. Even if a belief originated from outside of you, you allowed it to get inside your mind and stick. The thoughts inside your head stay there as a reminder of what you believe. Your mindset has to be strong enough that it does not allow anyone or anything to get inside of your head unless you allow it. Nothing can upset you and take you off course unless you allow it. Your mind is stronger than any muscle you have. Do not become a victim of your own mind. The only person in charge of your mind is you.

Your mind is your filter, for what you want to believe, do, think, see, feel, hear, etc. Your beliefs tell you everything. When you want to take action to do something, your belief filter tells you whether you should or not. It tells you whether it feels comfortable or not. Even if you think you believe something, your actions show what you truly believe. Your actions are the real truth. Your actions are you!

You are made up of all these different sides. You have a happy side, an angry side, a humorous side, a depressed side, a loving side, a giving side, an action-taking side, a lazy side, etc. All of these different facets of your personality make for a very complex self. You are a jigsaw puzzle made up of all these different pieces. You need to be in control of all of them. You want to strengthen the better pieces and weaken or keep in check those pieces that keep you from moving forward. Can you eliminate those bad pieces? Some people might be able to, but most people cannot. No doubt, that over time, the impact of the bad pieces can diminish, but you have to work to control them and keep them out of your way.

Your life changes the instant you make different decisions and take different actions compared to what you did in the past. You have to believe that what happened to you in the past has no bearing on what you can do now and in the future. You must get past yesterday and get to today. You must get past looking in the rearview mirror at what is already behind you and focus on what is around you at each moment. Learn from your past so you do not make the same mistakes again. Wisdom allows you to see true reality, not to see it the way you want it to be or think it is. Wisdom comes from learning from your mistakes and experiences, as well as other's mistakes and experiences.

For your next assignment, you will fill out your **Biography Sheet** (in the Appendix). This is self-discovery time. The sheet is full of questions. Questions allow you to get answers to who you are, where you have been, and where you are going. You may not know all the answers at this time and that is okay. For some of the questions the answers are always changing. You gain wisdom by seeking the answers to these questions. Kids are the best at asking questions. They never stop asking. As you get older, you lose your curiosity for life and stop asking questions. It is time to start asking questions again. These questions allow you to analyze and understand yourself. Who are you and what do you want? What are your strengths and weaknesses? What decisions and actions did you make or not make to end up where you are right now? Who and what, influenced you? What are your beliefs? What beliefs are limiting you? What beliefs are empowering you? What beliefs must you have to be successful? You have to have the right beliefs. Other people shaped most of your beliefs, so maybe they are not your real beliefs. Do you follow your own path, or do you try to please everyone else, by following his or her path? Are you living by what others believe, not necessarily what you believe? All of this can prevent you from becoming you. Are your beliefs limiting your success? Maybe others told you that you were not smart enough to succeed. Maybe they told you that you were not wealthy enough or attractive enough to succeed. Write down your beliefs and determine if you still believe in them. Question your beliefs to make sure each one is taking you in a successful direction; otherwise your beliefs are holding you back. You have been carrying these beliefs around all your life and it is time to determine if they are the right beliefs or not. You have to determine which beliefs to continue believing in and which ones to change or eliminate altogether.

You do not have to share your Bio with anyone unless you want to. This is personal information for your own use. This is a learning experience for you that should open your eyes as to who you are. Write down your answers. Start right now, rather than tomorrow. No excuses!

Dream It, Believe It, and Achieve It!

The most successful people in the world have different beliefs than everyone else. Your beliefs determine how you act and react to everything in your life. Most successful people started out like everyone else, but somewhere along the line, they changed their belief system. They started believing in big things instead of small things. If you are going to think and plan, think big and plan big. It takes the same amount of time, effort and belief. If you think big, you can achieve big things. If you think small, you cannot achieve big things. Beliefs are nothing more than feelings that something is certain to happen. If you walk out into the rain without an umbrella, you will get wet. That is a belief. Change your beliefs and you change your life. Do you believe you deserve to be successful? Successful people believe it. You have to believe it. They believe they can accomplish anything. They believe they can overcome their fears and any obstacles that get in their way. Each time they get knocked down, they believe they can get back up. First, and foremost they believe in themselves. If you do not believe in yourself, then why should anyone else believe in you? You cannot rely on others to build you up and provide you with belief. It has to come from within you, not from others. Since you just finished the **Bio Sheet** you know much more about yourself and it is time to get busy with the rest of your life. You did do the **Bio Sheet** right? If not, then get back to it!

You live your life based on what you believe. People's limited beliefs about themselves prevent them from achieving success. They usually settle for much less than they are capable of achieving. The Law of Attraction states that whatever you think about becomes reality. Your beliefs determine your reality. You listen to your inner voice. Whatever you tell yourself comes true.

You have to change your beliefs based on how you are going to live from this moment on. You should be asking yourself questions every day until you figure out how you want to live your life. Ask yourself the who, what, when, where and why of your life. Your beliefs determine your feelings and emotions for every decision you make. They determine your comfort zone. You have to change your old beliefs, and see the world differently than you did in the past, or you will have the same life you have now.

Do you believe you can accomplish whatever you want in your life? Most people do not believe they can. When you change your beliefs, you are sending different signals to your brain and reprogramming your mind. With different beliefs, you make different choices, and take different actions and get different results. Success starts with a dream and a belief. Who you truly are, is so much greater than who you think you are! Until your dreams and beliefs match up to your potential, you will never know how successful you can become.

Every person that has been successful in their life had doubts along the way, but they did not let those doubts stop them. Most people do not succeed because they have not succeeded in the past, and they feel they will get the same outcome again. They let their mind control them in a negative way. Their belief in failure is stronger than their belief in success.

The old saying, "Misery loves company" is very true. Those who do not follow their dreams may discourage you from yours. Do not let others influence you. Do not let them determine who you are. They are not you. Listen to what they have to say, but know that you are responsible for the final decisions. Your success is in your hands, not in their hands.

Look at the following limiting beliefs. These are the most common beliefs that prevent people from becoming successful.

1. **It is Impossible to do!** This is the most common belief. All you do is limit your potential by saying you cannot do something. Knowing that other people have accomplished great success helps you believe you can do it. You have to have good reasons for doing something so that you spend your time pursuing the right things. You need to change your beliefs that tell you that you cannot do something. You can accomplish anything. Once you achieve something you thought was impossible, it becomes easier to accomplish everything else.

2. **I do not have the Experience!** Experience is not the key to success. It is the person who wants it more! Demand more of yourself! Do more! Take more action! Focus more! Learn more! That is what counts. Experience has little to do with it. The high tech word is full of young and inexperienced success-

ful people. The sports world is full of inexperienced champions. Champions do not necessarily have more experience. The entertainment field is full of inexperienced, yet highly successful people. They simply wanted it more. They are successful because they bring energy, motivation and drive. They bring a mindset to the table that blows away the experience factor! You can be next.

3. **I do not have the Time!** What are you doing with your time? Everyone has 24 hours each day. Some people accomplish a great deal, while others accomplish absolutely nothing in those 24 hours. It is a matter of spending your time on the most important success-producing activities. Time is more important than money. You cannot buy time. Invest your time wisely and never wish your time away.

4. **The Blame Game.** Blaming everything on someone or something else like your parents, your significant other, your kids, your mortgage, your job, your boss, the economy, the world, the environment, your circumstances, etc., does not work. While you are wasting time playing the victim and playing the blame game, the rest of the people are moving forward. You must understand that you can only blame yourself from this point forward. Stop with the blame game! Do not play the victim, because it gets you nowhere. Someone has succeeded and yet has a better victim story than you do. It might sound good to you to blame other people or other things rather than yourself. Have you ever been in a car wreck? If it did not appear to be your fault then you blame the other person 100%, but you ended up in that place at that time because of your choices, so in a certain way it was your fault. If you had left your house/apartment ten seconds earlier, you would not have been in that spot to be in the wreck. So yes, the wreck was partly your fault. I know this is an extreme example and you can control most of what happens, but live

your life as if everything in your life is your responsibility. You cannot put the blame on anyone else unless you are under legal age, or mentally/physically unable to be responsible for your own well-being. Yes, there are certain exceptions to the blame game, but very few. Once you are able to make your own decisions you need to take charge of your life. The simple fact is that you prevent your own success. Do not blame anyone. You are responsible for your life.

5. **I do not have the Money.** Do not wait for others to come to your rescue by providing you with financial backing. It may not happen. Find a way to get the money. Work for it. Save for it. Do not buy that new car. Do not buy all those things that you do not need, until you have made it to where you want to be. Throw those credit cards in the trash. Drive past the mall and wave goodbye to it. Use your money wisely. You do not need much money to start a business, especially online. You do not need much money to make a film. You do not need much money to record your own songs and sell them online. You do not need much money to promote yourself, your skills, products, services and/or ideas.

6. **I am not Smart Enough.** Maybe you feel you are not smart enough to succeed. Maybe you were not a great student in school and therefore you feel that success is not going to happen for you. School curriculums are based on having to study and take tests in subjects that most likely held no interest for you. Maybe you hated math and history. When you find a subject you like, you have a different feeling for learning that subject. You will be an A+ student. Go educate yourself. Read books. Take classes. The internet is full of free education. If you do not own a computer, then go to any library and use their computers, or find a friend who has one. Get smart!

7. **I do not have the Talent.** It does not take talent to be successful. You can be the most talented person in the world, but

if you do not know what to do with that talent, then it will go to waste. Educating yourself replaces any lack of talent. You have to realize you have the potential, but you have to tap into that potential, and take action.

8. **Others.** Yes, other people will keep you from your dreams if you let them. Do not worry about what they think. It is your life not theirs.

Take all the limiting beliefs and excuses and throw them out the window! They don't work!

The Zone

You will not be completely comfortable in your life until you are doing what you want to be doing, and feeling what you want to be feeling. Until you reach that level of living, you must keep changing your comfort zone. Your beliefs determine how you feel, and how you feel determines your comfort zone and discomfort zone. Your links to comfort and discomfort determine the decisions you make, and the actions you take. You like to be comfortable and you make your decisions so that you remain comfortable. Everything you do is for the sole reason of staying in your comfort zone. It determines what you accomplish or do not accomplish. Some people like to refer to comfort and discomfort as pain and pleasure or heaven and hell. Call it what you want, but it drives you to make the decisions you make.

For most people, making changes makes them feel uncomfortable, so they choose to do nothing. That is the most comfortable choice. Your mind has been conditioned to stay in your comfort zone. Your comfort zone is unique to you and has been developed over your entire life. The only problem with your comfort zone is that it is not where success resides. Success lives outside the comfort zone. It is an emotional decision to get out of your comfort zone and venture out into the discomfort zone. In order to accomplish what you want, you are going to have to get out of your comfort zone and into your discomfort zone. If you do this often enough, making changes can become comfortable to you. Change becomes your new comfort zone. The discomfort zone is not as uncomfortable as you might think. You must keep expanding your zone.

You must force most people to change their life. They do not like their job, relationships, financial condition, health condition, and other areas of their life, but their belief is that making a change might be worse than staying exactly where they are. So they stay at the job, stay in the relationships, stay in their current life, even though they know they should change. They do not change until they have no other choice. Maybe they are fired from their job, or their relationship turns deadly, or they are financially ruined, or their health becomes life threatening, etc. The main problem is that things are usually just comfortable enough for them to keep things the way they are without making changes. Most employers pay you just enough to keep you from leaving. Most relationships are just good enough to keep you in it. Things are just tolerable enough to keep you from making changes. Making changes can be scary, so you avoid it at all costs, but it costs you dearly to avoid the new beliefs, decisions, choices, behaviors and actions that can lead you to success. It costs you in every area of your life.

Drug addicts usually do not stop until they hit rock bottom. They do not quit until they have no choice, either change or die. Many still do not change, and they pay the ultimate price. They overlooked what the long-term outcome would be and what it would cost them in terms of their health, wealth, relationships, career, and life.

Do you remember taking those timed tests in school? Taking tests are not anyone's example of a good time to begin with, but when you have the teacher calling out the minutes as they tick down to zero, the pressure increases. As the pressure increases, your thinking becomes progressively worse. It is like a thriller movie where the bomb is about to go off. The tension builds as the time ticks away. Too much pressure is not kind to your mind.

The problem with waiting until you **have** to do something, rather than **wanting** to do something, is that it puts you in a pressure situation. You are forced to do something once the pressure is on, and then you will do anything, even if it is the wrong thing, just to eliminate your discomfort. You probably know someone who made an even worse decision, while trying to get out of an initial bad situation, and things spiraled out of their control.

Pressure causes problems for all kinds of people. Job interviews are pressure situations. Some people do not handle interviews well. Some of the greatest entertainers cannot perform under the pressure of auditions and therefore, never make it. One of the funniest people I ever met never accomplished his dream of becoming a professional stand-up comic, because once he got on stage the pressure shut his mind down. He would walk on stage and instantly forget everything. It was painful for everyone to watch him crack under the pressure. He would have me in tears of laughter until he set foot on that stage, then I would be in tears of disbelief. You think much more clearly, when the pressure is the least. When the pressure and stress increase to the point of breaking you, you are not able to make the correct decisions.

Do not wait to make the decision to change something in your life. Do not wait until everything is against you. You need to be able to take action when you need to take action. Even the slightest delay can be disastrous, because the opportunity for success may be long gone. You always want to be ready to seize opportunities as they arrive. If you are always ready, then you never have to get ready.

Many people do not like public speaking. It is at the top of the fear list. For some, that fear traces back to their schooldays. Maybe they had one or more bad experiences back in school. If you have ever been to a grade school program where children perform on stage, there is always one child that cannot handle the pressure of the crowd watching them. That fear feels real, even if they made it up in their mind. Some people feel discomfort just thinking about public speaking. An uncomfortable feeling comes over them and their beliefs tell them what to do, which is to stay clear of public speaking. That fear recalls all of those feelings from that area in their mind where they hold all of their fear experiences. It opens up the floodgates and out come those feelings to put them in the discomfort zone.

All it takes is one bad experience to put a belief and feeling of fear into your mind. That is how your comfort/discomfort zone is developed. All areas of your life are full of fearful decisions. Fear tells you that you cannot do something. Fear tells you that failure is waiting for you. It causes you to give up trying. The key is to know that you can overcome your fears.

Successful people know they must get out of their comfort zone in order to move forward. They have very few, if any, limiting beliefs. They have more belief than fear. It is as simple as that. If they have a problem, they do not dwell on it like most people. They acknowledge the problem and start working on the solution. They look for the opportunity in the problem. They see the upside rather than the downside. They search for success not failure. It is time for you to move forward out of your comfort zone and past your fears.

Retrain

What will help you achieve success? Write down the new beliefs, feelings, actions, habits and behaviors that you need to have in order to be successful. These must replace the old ones that you need to eliminate. You have to have new beliefs that give you new feelings allowing you to take new actions to get new results. This allows you to develop new success habits and behavior. You cannot expect different results if you continue to follow the same old ways you have in the past. What will the new comfort be for replacing bad behavior with new behavior? What pleasure will you get from these new actions? Better financial security? Better relationships? Better physical and mental health? More time and money to give to others? More confidence? More of everything? Your mind has developed links or pathways to everything that brings you comfort and everything that brings you discomfort. You have certain experiences, situations, things, words, images, sounds, smells, etc., that trigger those comfortable and uncomfortable beliefs/memories, as if they were happening all over again. So how do you change your beliefs to allow you to take action and to achieve the success you want? You have to retrain your mind. In order to change your beliefs you have to change the feelings you link to your beliefs. If you cannot, then you fall back into the old beliefs and old behavior, because that is comfortable to you.

You must link comfort, happiness and great emotions to the beliefs, actions, habits, and behaviors that you need to have in your life. You must also link discomfort, pain and bad emotions to the beliefs, actions, habits, and behaviors that you must eliminate from your life. Determine what is stopping you from taking action. Fear? Rejection? Bad experiences? No experience? No confidence? No education? No time? No money? What has held you back? Write down all of your bad beliefs, actions, habits and behaviors that you have, and the feelings you link to them. Just the pain of regret of being where you are, and the wrong decisions you have made should be enough to make you feel uncomfortable and want to change. If specific events shaped your life and your decision-making, then revisit those events, one at a time. Close your eyes while doing this exercise. Relive that moment and feel those same emotions. See it, hear it, feel it, smell it, etc., all over again. Imagine the setting and the other people involved if you can. What feelings did you get as you replayed the event in your mind? Write everything down.

Write down what you will gain if you make the necessary changes and what you are losing if you continue to do what you have been doing. What is it costing you if you do not make the changes? By continuing the way things are, it costs you money, time, relationships, health, happiness, freedom and it may cost you your life.

Think of all the fears you have. For each one you have developed a fear link. Let us use public speaking as an example. In order to overcome that fear you must find a way to link comfort to public speaking. One way to accomplish this is to pull up a great memory that gives you a great feeling and then start visualizing that same feeling when you think of public speaking. Visualize yourself in the activity. Replace your feelings of fear, nervousness and embarrassment, with feelings of accomplishment, laughter, enjoyment, etc. Link those feelings of comfort to your new behaviors. If you fear meeting people, then link great feelings to meeting them. No matter what your fear is, you must overcome it by linking different thoughts to the activity, and then doing the activity until it feels comfortable and normal to you. Use images in your mind and actually place pictures in front of you that you link to that activity. If fear is keeping you from changing, then you have to be in the moment to keep things based in reality. How many times have you been afraid of doing something, and as soon as you did the activity, you realized there was nothing to fear? You made up the fear in your mind. Fear can protect you in certain situations, but it can also control you and stop you on your path to success.

Self-suggestion can be very useful. Self-suggestion is simply talking to yourself, which I know you do. Everybody does it. Talking and talking and talking until you embed the things you tell yourself in your mind and they become beliefs. People talk to themselves, but what most people tell themselves is negative. They tell themselves that they will fail. They embed those thoughts in their mind. From now on, talk to yourself in a different way. Talk to yourself in a positive manner. Tell yourself you can achieve anything you want and nothing can stop you.

You can also link a physical gesture to the feelings that you want for your beliefs. Try squeezing your thumb and index finger together, or making a fist when you think of great feelings. Do this over, and over, until the link has developed into a solid link. Practice this gesture every few minutes and after a short amount of time, it becomes natural. Athletes are constantly pumping their fist, because it gets them fired up. It provides them with an adrenaline rush. It gives them a great feeling of certainty about victory. Add in a vocal "yes" to the fist pumping and see if it fires you up. It puts you into a different state of mind. Go ahead and try it. Pump your fist and let out a yell, and see if it gives you a great feeling. When you think of public speaking, get excited! Pump yourself up with a fist pump and a yell and develop a positive link to that activity. I would not suggest you pump your fist and yell at the top of your lungs, as you are about to meet that special person in your life. It might be a comical moment, or you may scare them into running away from you. Mixing physical movement with deep breathing works to motivate you and get you into a positive mental state. Why do most gyms have upbeat music pounding through the speakers? It puts people in a state of mind that makes them want to work out. It gives them a great feeling to link to the activity of working out. Music is great for putting you into a successful state of mind. Use sounds, music, words, scents, physical gestures, deep breathing, etc., whatever it takes to help you link great feelings to the beliefs, actions, habits and behaviors you need.

Most athletes have a set routine. They go through the same mental and physical routine putting them into the right mental and physical state. Salespeople perform the same routine before they make a sales call. Investors use the same routine in the stock market. The top professionals in every industry have a set routine that makes them successful. Model yourself after them.

You ever wonder how free climbers can risk their life every time they execute a climb? Their body and mind feel that activity is normal. They believe in success. Their heart rate is normal as they risk their life. Their comfort zone is most people's discomfort zone. They would rather be in the arena than to be a spectator. Most people are spectators, even in their own lives.

You want to train your mind for maximum results just as you would pursue physical training to strengthen your physical body. Work out your muscles at the gym and you get stronger. Work out your mind and it gets stronger. It is the same concept. As soon as you stop behaviors that you want to rid yourself of, then those pathways or links in your mind weaken. As soon as you start behaviors that you want in your life, then those pathways or links strengthen. Repeating any behavior and linking great feelings to it carves out a new link in your mind. Make that link solid as a rock through repetition. You have to continue the behavior until it becomes natural to you. Most people try something for a short period and then quit because they do not see immediate results. Sadly, most of them quit right as they are on the verge of success. One more day, one more exercise, one more step, or one more repetition of the behavior and it would have worked.

You need to be honest with yourself. There are some beliefs and memories that you may never be able to link comfort to, but the possibility exists to prevent those beliefs and memories from stopping your pursuit of success. The bottom line is that you need to take a good look at all of your beliefs in all areas of your life and determine if you still believe in them. Even if you are successful in one area of your life it does not mean you are successful in all areas. Everyone has flaws in certain areas of their life. For almost every belief you have you can find someone who has the opposite belief. How can that be if your beliefs seem so certain to be right? Take a second look at your beliefs. Look at them and determine if they are still valid.

Your beliefs about what brings you comfort and discomfort determine the actions you take. The struggle between comfort and discomfort is a battle for everyone, but you can win the battle. For every action you take, your mind asks you whether it is going to bring comfort or discomfort. If you can find a way to link comfort to an action, then you will perform that action.

Motivation

Motivation is the internal force or feeling within you that drives you to do something. It drives you to take action. It is easy to get motivated, but difficult to stay motivated. Your emotions are the first motivating factor driving your behavior. Those emotions carry you for a short while, but then your feelings die down and you lose motivation. That initial passion is gone unless you achieve success to keep you motivated. That is why the pursuit and final achievement of any goal must have meaning for you. You have to enjoy doing what you are doing and have good reasons for doing it. If you do not believe in the goal you are chasing then it is almost impossible to maintain the pursuit. Remember, it is the feeling of comfort that drives you to do something, and discomfort that drives you to avoid something. Things you like, you have the natural motivation to pursue. Things you dislike, you avoid and struggle to find the motivation to pursue them. To be successful you must take certain actions you may not be motivated to do. Many artists do not like the business end of their industry. The artists that can mix their art with the business end are the most successful. You can hire others or partner with them to do those activities for you if you need to.

To stay motivated you must set daily goals that require taking daily action. Daily action keeps the momentum going, because you are being successful by accomplishing a little piece of the goal at a time, instead of having one big goal to achieve. Small accomplishments give you confidence. Daily goals develop daily behavior and discipline that motivate you for the long haul to success.

Attitude

Your attitude is very important. Beliefs and values make up your attitude. Does your attitude change as the situation changes? It is easy to have a great attitude when things are going great. The trick is to maintain that great attitude when things are not going so great by believing things will improve. You have to make it through the bad times to get to the good times. If you go into situations with a successful and positive attitude, then your chances for success increase. If you go into situations with a doubtful and negative attitude, then your chances for success decrease. Positive thinkers have more success than negative thinkers.

How can you have a more positive attitude? **Choose** your attitude. Decide to have a **positive** attitude. You have to work at developing a positive attitude just like you would work out at the gym. It is a mental workout. The more you work at it, the better you become at it. The more you become aware of your attitude, the more you can control it. You must realize that no one can change your attitude unless you allow it to happen. Everyone has buttons that can be pushed. Do not let people push your buttons and change your attitude. A quick trick to change your attitude is to change your facial expression by smiling. Try it. Also, change your physical posture by sitting/standing up straight and breathing deep. Try to have a bad attitude while smiling and laughing. I dare you. These are quick-fix attitude boosters. Work on your attitude!

The Right Thing

Your values are the way you live your life. Compare the way you live your life with the way you think you should live your life. Is there a difference? Ask yourself if the actions you are going to take will compromise you and your family, and others as well.

Most people who have long-term success in their life have stayed true to their values, maintained their integrity, and weathered the storms that came their way. Maintaining your true identity, while in pursuit of success, can be a tough road to follow. You do not want to do something you will regret, or become someone you are not. People will do anything to get money. People want success so badly they become whoever and whatever and they destroy themselves, as well as others.

Can you stay true to yourself when money and the shiny material things are sitting in front of you? If you cannot, then you may pay a steep price for your behavior. You may never recover and never reach the levels of success you dream about achieving. You know in your gut if what you are doing is the right thing to do. Do not put yourself in a compromising position just to be successful. If you will have to apologize to anyone for anything you are about to do then do not do it. In the end, the one thing you want to have left is your integrity.

Ask yourself these questions every time you are about to do something. Be sure you think about these questions so that you always do the right thing. The answers should be "yes" to 1-4 and "no" to 5.

1. Will it benefit you and everyone else?
2. Will it strengthen your relationships/friendships?
3. Will you feel proud afterwards?
4. Will it move you in the right direction towards accomplishing your goals?
5. Will there be a negative impact for anyone?

Decision and Change

Success is a decision. Your daily decisions impact what happens in your life and the lives of others. You may not even realize you are making decisions. Every step you take is a decision to go in a particular direction. Everything you do is a decision made by you. You must become aware of the decisions you make, so that you make decisions to be successful. You have to make the decision to step forward and take the lead in your life. Take that step. It leads to big things. You cannot wait for anyone else to make decisions for you. They are interested in their own success, not your success. If you allow other people to make decisions for you then they are in control of you.

Opportunities have always been available to you and it is simply a matter of making the decision to take advantage of them. Look for opportunities in places you never thought to look before.

Your daily decisions move you closer to success or further away from success. That is why you must fill out the **Daily Log**. It shows what you do every minute of your day. It shows what decisions you make and whether those decisions are moving you in the right direction. Write down the decisions you make each day and the decisions you let others make for you. Are you ready to change?

Change leads to something better. The sooner you change, the sooner you achieve your dreams. It is very easy to decide. Decide right now!

Planting Seeds

Do you pay attention to what you put into your mind as much as you pay attention to what food and drink you put into your stomach? Or do you allow information into your mind without paying any attention to what is going in there? If you know something is not good for you, do you still allow it into your mind anyway? You need to be conscious of what you put into your mind. All ideas start up there. Anything that you repeatedly suggest to yourself will embed itself into your subconscious mind and drive your behavior. You have to direct your thoughts toward what you want. The way to plant seeds into your mind is to use self-suggestion by telling yourself the correct thoughts and beliefs you need to have. Use words that describe the present situation and contain the words, "I am" or "I feel." They show action. "I am confident" or "I feel confident" and "I am changing my habits" and "I am working out." You do not want to use the past or future tense such as "I was" or "I will." As an example, comparing the phrases "I was a smoker" to "I am not a smoker" shows how a slight change in words can have a huge impact on your success of remaining a non-smoker. The first phrase tells your mind that you still have the potential to be a smoker, whereas the second phrase eliminates smoking from your mind altogether. Stay with the present. Stay with what is happening now. You must repeat these suggestions until they take root in your subconscious mind and develop links. Your subconscious mind acts on the new ideas you have planted. Remember, the Law of Attraction states that whatever you think about, you attract and become.

Plant your who, what, when, where, and why into your mind. Focus on them and your mind drives you to act upon them and achieve them. You are simply planting your plan of action in your mind. Your mind is at work 24 hours a day. Your mind never sleeps. It is as simple as when you tried to remember the name of a restaurant, movie or person, but you could not remember it. Then later it pops into your head seemingly out of nowhere. That was not an accident. That was your mind working on the seed that you planted. Your mind works for you or against you, depending on what you plant inside of it. This is not an overnight process. Things take time to grow, but they grow when you feed them properly. Your mind is simply the garden where you plant whatever it is that you want to grow.

If you plant defeating thoughts and ideas inside your head, then that is exactly what grows. Resist putting negative, self-defeating thoughts into your head. They are dream killers. Most people put negative suggestions into their mind. They are afraid of embarrassing themselves. They worry about what others think or say about them. Those negative thoughts dominate their mind. Family, friends and complete strangers love to fill your head with the wrong ideas. Do not allow others to put the wrong thoughts into your head. Those ideas get planted into your head if you allow them in. Even the smallest amount of doubt in your head causes you to lose your confidence.

You must plant the right seeds by telling your mind the right thoughts. Start out each day by commanding great positive feelings rather than negative feelings. Determine how you want to feel from the moment you wake up. Do not let anyone or anything impact how your day goes. You are the gatekeeper. Your conscious mind does not allow the wrong ideas and thoughts into your subconscious mind unless you allow it. Use the following list of **Success Thoughts** to help you. Make your own list if you like. Spend some quiet time each day and ponder these thoughts.

Success Thoughts

The following list is for daily reading. Read it several times each day. Keep it visible so that you are continually reminded how to live each day. Plant these seeds into your mind.

1. Yesterday is gone. There is no going back! Look forward move forward.
2. Look at life differently than you did yesterday.
3. Live every minute. Be enthusiastic about life. Love rain as well as sunshine.
4. Be friendlier, more excited, and more persuasive.
5. Enjoy working with people. Be interested in them.
6. Smile and laugh. It changes your attitude instantly.
7. When you have 100 reasons to cry, find one reason to smile and laugh.
8. Find humor in almost every situation.
9. Do not make up excuses, because there are no excuses.
10. No complaining.
11. Admit your mistakes, learn from them and avoid making them again.
12. You will fail and face rejection. Learn from those experiences.
13. Program your mind for success by visualizing yourself being successful. See what you are, not what you were.
14. Focus on your passions.
15. Believe in yourself and others.
16. Expect to be successful.
17. Do not fear the fear. Most fears are made-up in your mind.
18. Stick to the basics.
19. The little things make the difference.
20. Success is simple, common sense.

21. Make the complex simple, not the simple complex, by taking complex ideas/plans and breaking them down into small simple steps of action.
22. Spend time with people you can learn from, profit from and have fun with.
23. Keep clutter out of your life.
24. Focus your energy and time on the most important activities.
25. Make a habit of breaking your habits. Develop successful habits.
26. Do not take no for an answer. Keep asking.
27. Ask why not, instead of why.
28. Hope is not a plan. Do not hope success happens make it happen.
29. Walk the talk by holding yourself accountable and doing what you say you are going to do.
30. Decide to take charge, because no one else can do it for you.
31. Be consistent in your performance, attitudes, etc.
32. Be flexible.
33. Be honest.
34. Be kind.
35. Be motivated.
36. Be loyal.
37. Be prepared.
38. If they can do it, you can too!
39. Give it everything you have and never give up!
40. Think big, plan big and take big action.
41. Think possibilities not failures.

42. Think solutions not problems.

43. Focus on the positives, not the negatives.

44. Challenge yourself daily. Demand more of yourself. When you have gone as far as you can go, you can usually go further!

45. Your potential is unlimited. Tap into it and reap the benefits.

Learning

Learn from everything and everyone, and then teach others to benefit as well. Learning keeps you young and interested in life. Learning includes understanding how to use knowledge. Learning teaches you how the world works. Improve your mindset and skill set by constantly being in learning mode. The more you know the more action you can take. Seek out material on subjects that help you progress and increase your chances of success.

Mentors are a great source for learning. Model your behavior after positive and successful people. Seek them out. Contact them and ask them if you can have ten minutes of their precious time to interview them on what makes them successful. They might give you thirty minutes of their time, or they might tell you to get lost, but you still must ask. Choosing the right mentor is the key. You do not have to follow the people who look good, dress sharp, smell like money, drive the most expensive car, and live in the large estate. They may be struggling to pay for all of it. It may be all for show.

Learning is leverage. Learning helps you know what to do, how to do it and when to do it. It gives you the confidence to succeed and when you achieve any success, it builds momentum. Learn something every day by reading, observing and asking. Observation is a key to learning. Sometimes you have to jump off the merry-go-round of life and observe how it works. Make learning a daily activity for the rest of your life.

Rejection

In order to be successful in life, you have to put yourself out into the world where rejection is an everyday occurrence. Rejection happens, so prepare for it. Rejection is the main reason most people sit at home afraid to pursue personal relationships, afraid to look for a job and afraid to pursue their dreams, because actually going out into the world means facing rejection. It is the main reason most people give up trying altogether. Rejection is not a reason to give up on your dreams. Most successful people go through a lot of rejection.

Rejection is one of the most difficult psychological barriers to overcome, because it is like a mental punch in the stomach. Rejection makes you feel like you are not worthy and not acceptable to them as a person. People want acceptance and to be liked. Rejection always feels like a personal attack, even though it might be your skills, product, service, idea, song, film, book, etc., that is being rejected, rather than you as a person. When you put anything out there in front of the world, expect to get the best and worst of everything. Those praising you today might criticize you tomorrow. As you become more successful the criticism increases, so expect it and be prepared for it. You must realize that if a person does not know you personally, then they are criticizing who they think you are, or what they think you represent.

Discrimination is another form of rejection that exists. People might treat you unfairly based on your age, looks, disability, race, religion, gender, beliefs, etc. Expect it and keep moving forward, and do not let anyone stop you. Find people who do believe in you. They are out there waiting for you to arrive. Prove to them, you are as good as advertised.

What are your beliefs about rejection? How do you respond to it? You cannot let rejection defeat you or let it change your behavior.

Deal With It - Rejection

How you react to personal and professional rejection determines how well you are able to move past it and stay on your success path. The rule is not to set yourself up for rejection by thinking everything will go according to your plan. Do not expect too much too soon. Be reasonable. Remember, you cannot control everything and everyone.

Rejection is only one person's opinion. You have your opinion and they have their opinion. The reason for your rejection could be as simple as the other person was in a bad mood that day. Maybe it was not what they were interested in at that time. They may be interested the next time you are in contact with them. Rejection happens to everyone, so you are not alone. Develop a thick skin so each rejection becomes easier to handle. It is never easy, but you can handle it.

Stay focused on the end result. Be flexible and understand the possible outcomes that may occur on your road to the end result. You only have to find the right person to say "yes" to you. **Never** stop looking. By them saying "no," it only means you have not given them a reason to say "yes." They are telling you that you can do better. When you are truly ready, everyone says "yes." Some like to think of it as a numbers game, meaning that if you contact enough people, then sooner, or later one will say "yes." You are doing something wrong if rejection is the normal response you are receiving.

Be professional in the face of rejection and criticism. Do not let your emotions rise to the surface in the presence of the person or group rejecting you. Never lose your temper in front of them. It is a small world so you do not want to burn any bridges by saying or doing something unprofessional. You never know when you will run across their path again. You may end up becoming the best of friends and partners in business. Give yourself a moment before responding to anyone when your feelings are boiling to the surface. If you are not professional, then all you do is show them that they made the right decision in rejecting/criticizing you.

Do not keep your personal feelings bottled up inside. Discuss your feelings with family and friends. Rejection hurts. It may be drumming up old feelings from your past so you need to talk about it with someone.

Step back and analyze why the rejection might have happened. What is working and what is not? What is within your control and what is out of your control? Try to be as objective as possible to determine the reason behind your rejection. You can learn so much from rejection if you can determine why it occurred.

You must separate your personal rejection from your business rejection. If the rejection is from a personal relationship, you must realize that you might not be a match for them. It is time to move forward. There are billions of people in this world, so you just might be able to find someone else. You cannot be at the mercy of others for your happiness. Your validation comes from **you being you**, not from you being someone others want you to be. You must be able to listen to people say "no" without you giving up. Your strong mindset enables you to overcome rejection and keep you moving in the right direction.

Separation

No matter what you choose to do in your life there is plenty of competition. Successful people are able to separate themselves from the competition by getting better at what they do, so in reality competition only exists for those in the herd fighting for the leftovers. Watch any nature program and you will see a member of the herd eaten every day. The leaders of the herd are long gone by the time the lions show up looking for lunch. Unfortunately, people have a herd mentality. They like to stay in a group, because they feel safer in a group. People like to play it safe. There is that comfort zone getting in the way again. Being a member of a group puts you in that comfort zone, but that comfort zone is a danger zone for success. Members in a group feel secure, but they are not secure. They do what everybody else is doing, and avoid the discomfort zone and avoid success.

You must rise above the level that keeps you in competition with the majority of the people. You have to rise above the herd by raising your standards beyond where they are now. Your edge separates you from the crowd! Your edge is what makes you different from everyone else. You are one of a kind. No one else thinks like you. No one else sees the world like you. No one else can offer what you can. You have to discover and use your uniqueness, because it sets you apart from everybody else. That is your edge. You have to get out there and use your edge! Have fun! Be alive! Get away from what everyone else is doing. What makes you unique? What makes you different? What makes you, you? Use the **Bio Sheet** to write down what you think separates you from the competition. If you are not sure, then it is time to discover it.

Failure Is Great

Failure is a guarantee. You will experience failure! Let me repeat that. **YOU WILL EXPERIENCE FAILURE!** You have to plan for it so when it happens, you are ready. If you own a car or truck, you carry a spare tire. That is a plan for failure. Buying car insurance is a plan to prevent financial failure in case of an accident. Getting into great physical shape is a plan to prevent failure of your health.

Most people do not take action because of their fear of failure, but they do not realize they are failing by not taking action. They slowly, but surely, fail over a long period of time, by not doing what they should be doing on a daily basis. I call it Slow Failure, because it happens over their life without them even knowing it. They do not notice Slow Failure, because it is not one big failure. They wake up decades later and realize they did not take the proper steps to achieve their dreams.

The great news about failure is that there is more than one type of failure. Besides Slow Failure, think about the terms Temporary

Failure and Total Failure. Temporary Failure means temporary setbacks. It is impossible to fail if you keep trying. The only real way to fail is to quit! When you quit, that is Total Failure. Game over!

Most success comes out of failure. Thomas Edison failed 3,000 times before he found the proper filament for his commercial version of the light bulb. That is a lot of temporary failure. What if Edison had given up and quit? Many of the wealthiest people in the world have lost everything at one point or more in their life. Have you ever watched a boxing match? Every boxer gets hit. Every time they get hit that is failure, but they keep on fighting. Baseball players are considered great if they can bat 300, meaning they get a hit three out of every ten times at bat. They fail 70% of the time. Most people would give up if they failed 70% of the time. If you never fail then you are not trying. You are not going for it. You are avoiding risks and challenges and playing it safe. You are hiding in your comfort zone. You cannot be successful if you play it as safe as most people play it.

You must have alternate paths to achieve success. Failure is simply one path that did not work. You have eliminated that path and it is time to move onto the next one. Be flexible. Do not get locked into one way, one plan or one approach. Most people have one plan, and as soon as it goes wrong they give up. They are not mentally prepared for temporary failure so the end result becomes total failure. When you have moments of failure along the way, what are you going to do? Quit or keep going? Most people focus on their failures and give up just when they are about to achieve success.

Learn from your failure and keep going! Failure is actually progress unless you keep making the same mistakes over again. Each time you fail you become smarter and better prepared for your next action. Failure makes you ready.

Handling failure is extremely important. In order for you to grow and be more successful, you have to try new things, and when you do, there are moments of temporary failure. Think about what you are going to do before you do it, and think of the possible outcomes. Be prepared for all outcomes to help eliminate temporary failure.

Pain

Success takes work. Unfortunately, most people seem to be allergic to work. They look for and take the easy way out. Work is too painful for them. It is not physically painful, but mentally painful, when they do not see instant success. It is uncomfortable for them and no one likes to be uncomfortable. You have to be ready to go through some tough stuff along the way to success.

The pain involved in the pursuit of dreams is nothing compared to the long-term pain of not pursuing your dreams. You do not want to get old wondering if you could have accomplished your dreams. Can you deal with the thought that you stopped short of trying? There are millions of people looking back on their lives wishing they had chased after their dreams. Do not be a member of that group. You will regret it. The pain of regret lasts a lifetime. The pain of rejection, pain of discipline, pain of hard work and pain of sacrifice, are much less painful than the pain of regret. If you do not take that first step then you will suffer the pain of regret. You might already be suffering from the pain of regret knowing the things you should have done up to this point in your life. Regret for not living up to your potential. Regret for not achieving your dreams. Regret for giving up or not even trying.

When you set daily goals, you must achieve them. If you do not achieve them, then you have to feel the pain. That pain makes you work. That pain drives you to success. It has to be painful for you to look in the mirror at night and tell yourself you did not achieve your daily goals. You cannot feel good about missing your goals. Did you give it your all? Did you have something left over at the end of the day? Could you have done more? If so, you did not for some reason. It is not okay to stop short of giving it everything you have. The pain will drive you to change. An addict cannot quit until they feel the pain. Pain drives you to change whatever you are doing that is causing the pain. You cannot hide from it. It is always there until you face it and eliminate it!

When you feel the pain you shift your mindset and transform into the person you are capable of being.

Commitment

Most people do not hold themselves accountable for their commitments. Meeting commitments means doing what you said you were going to do. Most people miss their commitments because they are irresponsible and unable to prioritize their activities.

How do you feel when you miss your commitments to yourself, to your family, and to others? Better yet, how do you feel when others miss their commitments to you? If you can look at yourself in the mirror and feel good about missing your commitments, then you do not believe in your commitments.

Remember, it is not whether you can or you cannot do something, it is whether you will or you will not. When you do what is necessary, that is commitment. You can always do something, but will you? Simple question with a huge impact! Transform your life by changing your mindset from should to **must**. Instead of thinking you should do something, your new mindset tells you that you must do something. Must is a different mindset altogether. Must is a different way of thinking and a more powerful position than should or could or would. Most people talk about doing something rather than doing it. Talk, talk, and more talk! You should do this, and you could do that, or you would do this and that, but you did not! You were going to work on your new business during lunch, but your friends asked you to go out to lunch so you did not work on it. You were going to go to the gym, but. You were going to read a book in your area of interest, but. You were going to write a new song, but. Excuses, excuses, excuses. Take what you should, could and would do and make them things you **must** do. You must get them done. What you **do** tells the real story. What you say means nothing.

Warning! You do not want to get so obsessed with your goals that you lose balance in your life. You must go after your goals, but maintain a healthy and balanced life. Obsession can add so much pressure that it leads to failure. The sports world shows us how putting too much pressure on ourselves can result in failure.

Commit to making something big happen every single day because this creates momentum. Momentum creates excitement and energy that carries you through the rest of your day. Live out of that commitment. Committing means you have no choice but to do whatever it is you commit to doing. As soon as you commit, you have to hold yourself accountable for those commitments. At the end of each day you know whether or not you have lived up to your commitments. Look at the facts. Did you do what you said you were going to do? Yes or no? There are no partial commitments. Your actions met your commitments or they did not.

What will you commit to doing each day, each week, each month and each year? You cannot be successful without committing. Commitments take over your mind and get planted. They are seeds that grow. You do whatever you commit to doing. Your mind keeps working on your commitments while you sleep.

Tell people about your commitments. When you tell the world what you are up to, they look for you to accomplish those things. It puts pressure on you. Pressure brings a sense of urgency to your life. Add pressure to carbon and you get diamonds. Add pressure to your goals and it may bring diamonds to you. Success requires commitment and pressure.

Focus

You get what you focus on. It is important to focus your attention on the right things. If you focus on failure, you get failure. If you focus on success, you get success. Focus means putting energy into something. Focus on the bad side of someone and you see them as bad. Focus on the unattractive side of someone and you see them as unattractive. Focus on the positive and attractive side of them and that is what you see. Focus on the solution instead of the problem and you get the solution to the problem. Focus on what you want and it drives you to get it.

Maintaining focus is one of the most difficult mental skills to develop, especially when you are bombarded by rejection, failure, distractions, seeds of doubt, etc. You must have discipline to stay focused for the long term. It is easy to stay focused for the short term, but long term is another story, because prolonged focus on the same issues/things/tasks seems routine, and boredom sets in. That is why you have to have the right purpose for what you are doing. It keeps you interested for the long haul. It keeps you from becoming bored and jumping to something new and more appealing. To achieve long-term results you must focus your efforts on the smallest number of key activities that generate the greatest results. Focus on what needs to be accomplished each step of the way. It is no different than driving down the road to your destination. You have to pay attention the whole way. If you focus only on the end destination, you may run off the road or worse. In time, you move forward towards the end goal. You have to know your limits on what you can accomplish each day. Working on too many activities spreads you too thin to be effective in achieving any of your goals.

Placing physical reminders in clear view helps you stay focused. Put the word "FOCUS" in big, bold letters everywhere you can, to remind you to focus. In time, focusing becomes part of your subconscious, which drives automatic behavior.

The term often used for being focused is "being in the moment" or "being there." It is a simple concept. You can only focus on one thing at a time. When you are at work, be at work. When you are with your family, be with your family. When you are on vacation, be on vacation. Are you often in a conversation with someone and you cannot recall what he or she was talking about? This means you are not being in the moment. You are not listening to that person. You are there physically, but your focus is somewhere else. If your focus wanders then you cannot be using your time properly. Focus on the right thing at the right time.

Are you able to change your focus when you need to? When things are not going your way, you have to change your focus to find that path towards success.

Sports prove how important focus can be at crucial moments. Focus only on the current play. Do not focus on the score, or what just happened, or what might happen. Stay in the moment. See yourself performing exactly what you want to have happen. **Focus**.

Discipline

Discipline is simple. It is the ability to do what you must do on a daily basis. You must do something every day to move you closer to achieving your dreams/goals. At first, you might not see any progress, but it is happening. There is a lag time between action and success. Most people quit when they do not see instant progress. Know that success is coming.

No Excuses

Successful people do not make up excuses. Excuses do not work. People love to make up excuses so they do not have to try to succeed. You are either making progress or making excuses! You cannot do both. The amount of success you want to achieve is up to you.

Living a Great Life

The ultimate success is living a great life and helping others live a great life. Be productive, be a great friend and family member, and be an inspiration to others. It does not mean making the most money or living in the biggest house or driving the most expensive car, etc. It is so much more than that. It is time to stop wasting time. Live every moment. If you live life to the fullest, it shows up in everything you do. It is magical. You are a force. Fulfill your dreams, and the dreams of others.

Conclusion

In order for you to achieve success in both your personal life and your professional life, you first have to develop a success mindset. Only then, can you make the right decisions and take the right actions on a daily basis. Think the right thoughts and make the right choices every day. **Success is a daily activity.** Start now!

2
Success Management

"You have to manage your life, because no one else will."

Welcome to the Management Material. This is where you develop new habits and plan daily actions that best utilize your time to change your life, both personally and professionally. You must manage your life effectively and efficiently to be successful. Successful people are brilliant at the basics, and the basics begin by managing each day. Either you run each day or each day runs you.

Managing Time

The clock is ticking. In order to explode your success you have to be able to get better results in less time than you have been getting. You must master time. By properly managing your time, you are able to find hours of extra time each day that never seemed to be available. It is as if you are creating time.

Once you write down what you want then you have to plan out the actions to take in order to achieve it. You filled out the **Daily Log** to show how you use your time. Did you fill it out? Great! Now use a new copy of the **Daily Log** to create your new day, as it should be. You must plan it out, because it is so easy to spend/waste your time doing something else. Find purpose in everything you do. If you cannot, then you should be doing something else.

For each minute of your time, there are several questions to ask yourself.

1. Am I learning anything from what I am doing?
2. Will this activity help me achieve success?
3. Would I be better off doing something else?

Set aside periods/blocks of time (time blocking) each day, for certain activities, but they have to be the right activities. There is not enough time to do everything so you must prioritize. Schedule one activity per block of time. You either block your time or waste your time. Develop time blocking habits so you do not end up with time wasting habits. Protect that time. Do not let anything interrupt you. If you are working on your new business, only work on it. If you are supposed to be prospecting for new customers, prospect. If you are writing your new song, book, or film script, then write. If you are looking for a job, only look for a job. If you are with your family, be with your family. If you are studying about investing, or some other subject, study. Do not answer the phone, do not email, do not text, do not surf the net, do not watch TV, do not eat, do not do anything else but the activity you have time blocked to do. If you are supposed to be checking your email, then check your email. Block your time for your activities.

Look at the following list of time wasters to determine if you are guilty of any of these. The **Daily Log** that you filled out might include some of these. These happen because you allow them to happen. You have to be in control of your actions and your environment to eliminate the following time wasters.

1. **Interruptions** from people, phone calls, email, texts, surfing the internet, meetings, watching TV, reading, playing games, etc. Make it clear to people that when you are working, you are not to be interrupted. Make calls between certain times of the day. Do not answer the phone if you have time blocked for

other activities, unless the phone call is related to the activity you are working on, or is an emergency. Meetings need to have an agenda, and start and finish on time.

2. **Lack of a Clear Daily Plan**. You must have a written plan of action with deadlines/schedules that must be met.
3. **Lack of Focus** on the right activities. You must prioritize the activities that bring you the best results and understand why you are doing what you are doing.
4. **No Leverage**. No delegation of activities. At some point, you might need to hire an assistant or outsource things that need to be done. If you are concerned about the cost, or are nervous about delegating activities, start slowly. You may be thinking that you cannot afford to hire someone, but maybe you can. It costs you time to perform these activities yourself. Pay them so it frees up your time for more important activities and increases your chances of success.
5. **No Processes** for your life. Processes are simple step-by-step plans. Without processes, you have to continually reinvent the wheel each time you do something. This causes you to waste time, make mistakes and miss deadlines. Write down the steps for activities you do, that have multiple steps.
6. **Procrastination** deserves its own section.

Procrastination

Some people are born procrastinators. No matter how much or how little they have to do, they always seem to find a reason for postponing what needs to be done. They always find something else to do in place of what they should be doing. They avoid taking action. Procrastinators usually know what they need to do, but doing it is the problem. They talk a good game, but they never play the game. Most people procrastinate before they even start their day. Their alarm clock goes off in the morning and they reach over and hit the snooze button. They hit it several more times before finally dragging themselves out of bed after wasting 30 minutes.

Why do people procrastinate? Blame it on the comfort zone. Listed below are the top reasons people procrastinate.

1. **Fear of Failure**. This is the number one reason and is most often the deciding factor in the other reasons listed below. This includes the fear of being rejected, embarrassed, and ridiculed. Fear enters your mind when you are not prepared for what you are about to do, and/or you are putting yourself in a new situation where you have no experience, and/or because you failed in the past. Most fear is not real. It is all in your mind and your mind is allowing this negative vision to become your belief. You believe you are going to fail. Doubt takes over your mind and stops you dead in your tracks. You have to push forward. Successful people make mistakes all the time, but they do not let it stop them. Making mistakes is part of the game. Play the game.

2. **Lack of Interest**. The majority of people in this world are not in love with what they are doing in most areas of their life. Lack of interest kills motivation. If you have passion for something then you owe it to yourself to go for it. Find passion in all areas of your life.

3. **Defiance**. Some people simply do not want to work. Defiance is normally based on a person's dislike for what they are doing. If you are defiant, it is time to determine what you really want to do with your life.

4. **Perfection**. Perfection is one of the most common causes of procrastination. You think you do not know enough or do not have everything exactly the way you want it prior to taking action. The perfect moment rarely comes along. You may never be 100% ready. At some point, you have to go for it.

Trust that you are smarter and more capable than you think you are. Stop trying to be perfect. Take action. You learn more by taking action than by over-thinking everything prior to taking action.

5. **Fear of Success**. This cause is less common, but no less disabling. Success can bring on a new set of problems that many people are not ready to handle. People fear success will change them or change other people's attitudes towards them. Your family and friends, and others may change because of your success. Be ready for it. They may think you have changed and it may only be their new reality of you. They look at you differently. They may want those shiny material things and/or money that you can now afford to give them. Plenty of people want to ride your coattails. You have to remain the same person. Stay humble. Think of all the good you can do with your success. Think of all the people you can help. Helping others should be your end goal. Enjoy your success, but give back as well.

Overcoming Procrastination

The best way to rid yourself of procrastination is to break up your goals into daily goals/steps. If you look at each goal as one big task, it can often be an overwhelming thought.

If you are a procrastinator, try following a simple rule. Every day, pick the most important goal/step from your list and do it first. Tackle difficult tasks head on. After a couple of weeks of this, you will procrastinate less.

Set yourself up to win every single day by focusing on the activities that help you achieve your goals. Block your time. You can be effective and efficient at managing your time, but if you spend your time on the wrong activities, then you are wasting time.

Balance

You must have proper balance in your life, between business, day job (if different than business), family and friends, vacation/celebration/relaxation, hobbies, learning, health (mental and physical), spirituality (depends on your beliefs), giving back, etc. Spend too much time in any one area and the other areas suffer. Nothing brings on stress and health issues quicker than an out-of-balance life. If you love working 70 hours per week and it is fine with everyone else in your life, then continue. If it poses problems, then you have to balance things out. You have to set rules. Do not make yourself available 24/7. You are not an open-all-night convenience store. Sometimes you have to say "no" to people. Turn off your cell phone. Balance your life by managing your time.

Use the **Daily Log** to determine the number of hours you spend on the different areas of your life. Is your life in balance? If it is not in balance then you have to determine what needs to be changed. Determine the areas that need more attention and the areas that you can cut back on. Start thinking about how you can get more things done by paying someone else to do them for you. Maintain your balance.

Habits

Successful people have great habits that drive their continued success. Success comes from changing bad habits into great habits. Developing successful habits changes your mindset to a success mindset. It is time to break away from the old way of doing things. Break out of your comfort zone and change your habits.

You have to ask yourself what you are committed to doing. Do you want great success, or do you want others to have all the success? It is up to you. Doing more of the same thing gets you more of the same thing. Spending more time following your old habits can create more success, but you want more success by doing better, not by working more. You lose balance in your life by spending more time following old habits.

In order to change your habits you have to be aware of what your habits are in the first place. You gained an awareness of your habits when you filled out your **Daily Log**.

The goal is to cut out everything that wastes your precious time during your day. Most people waste 1-4 hours every day on non-productive activities. Think how much you can accomplish with that extra amount of time available to you.

If you simply pay attention to what you do every day, then you can instantly change your habits. For some people it is impossible to try and change all of their habits at once. Find your worst habits and start with them. Start **right now**, not later today or tomorrow!

Step-By-Step

You live your life following step-by-step habits whether you realize it or not. You use them for work, for fun, for whatever you do on a daily basis. Every day you wake up and go through the same steps. The steps are a process. If you change the steps you feel a bit out of sync, because it goes against your daily process that you normally follow. The way to change your bad habits is to interrupt them. In order to change your life you have to interrupt your normal life. It boosts your energy, because your body is more alive wondering why things are not the same. It takes you out of your comfort zone. It is as simple as taking a different route to work than you normally take. It wakes you up!

You need to develop step-by-step processes for activities that you repeat, especially for your business. Look at your habits and find the best process for each one. Write down the steps. To change your habits use the following steps.

1. **Become Aware** of your habits. Make a list of the bad and the good.
2. Write down the **New Habits** that you want in place of your bad habits.

3. Write down the **Steps** for each new habit.
4. **Link Pain** to the current habit/behavior, and **Pleasure** to the new replacement habit/behavior. Where you are right now causes you pain. Your pleasure is the success you achieve when you change.
5. **Take Action** by following your new habits until they become natural and automatic. Repetition is how you develop a habit.
6. **Place Reminders** of the new habits everywhere.
7. **Review and Improve** your habits on a daily basis.

It takes approximately 3-4 weeks to eliminate old habits and develop new habits. You do not need a process for everything in your personal life. You are not a robot. For your professional life, if you have everything in writing, then you can follow your processes without letting your emotions make decisions for you. People who do not have written processes for running their life may end up making rash decisions based on emotions. Developing successful processes allows you to use them over and over, duplicating your success time and time again. Do not be so rigid in following a process that you lose all chance for flexibility and improvement.

Creating Your Future - Goal Setting

A goal is a dream that you take action on in order to achieve. The goal does not determine the way you will achieve it. It is an outcome or target to hit. Goals are not things you try to do, or things you want to do, they are things you **commit** to doing, because you have the desire and passion to accomplish them.

You must act with urgency by setting daily goals. If you set goals further out into the future then you have no pressure to achieve those goals, and days pass by without you taking action. Developing a plan and sticking to that plan is required for long-term success. If you plan each day, you know exactly what will happen that day. Your plan has to be legitimate. Do not take it easy on yourself. The easy way does not get you the results. If success were easy, then everyone would be successful. You are inventing/creating your own future. You are controlling your destiny. No one else should control it. You are your own CEO. You are the President of You!

The following steps move you from merely thinking about your goals, to taking action to achieve your goals.

1. **List Goals**. Simply make a list of the top goals in all areas of your life.

2. **Prioritize Goals**. Take your list of goals and list them in order of priority, so you direct your time and energy to the right goals. If you listed 100 goals, which ones are the most important?

3. **Get Specific**. The wording of the goal and the expected outcome should be clear and concise. The more specific you get with your goals, the easier it is to take the steps needed to achieve them, and to monitor and record your progress. A financial goal may be to increase your income by a specific amount. A physical exercise goal may be to walk two miles each day. All the details for each goal must be in writing. List the reason you want the goal, the schedule or timeline for the goal, the way to measure the progress of each goal, the required people and equipment for each goal, etc. These are explained below, in greater detail.

4. **Reason**. For each goal, you must determine why you want to achieve that goal. Why is each goal important to you? What value is added to your life? How does this goal help others as well? The more reasons you list for your goals, the more motivated and dedicated you are towards achieving them.

5. **Time Limit**. All goals must have a deadline for completion. Placing deadlines on your goals puts pressure on you to accomplish them.

6. **Conflicting Goals**. Do any of your goals conflict with each other? There will be conflicts for your time, focus, money, life balance, etc. Life has a way of getting in the way of your goals. Spending money on business goals may conflict with spending money on personal goals. Maybe your religious goals conflict with the business goals you want to pursue. All conflicts must be resolved.

7. **Just The Facts**. All goals have to be measurable. Set goals and measure the results. If you want to increase your income, you must know how much of an increase you want. You want to double your client list by what date? If you want more vacation, how much more? You want to help a homeless person, but how? You want to be a better person by changing and doing what? The goals have to be detailed. Think in terms of numbers, costs, and deadlines that can be used to show your progress. The facts do not lie. Either you made progress and met your goals or you did not. Intentions do not matter. Hope does not matter. Emotions do not matter. The numbers matter. The facts matter.

8. **Requirements**. What do you need to achieve each goal? Do you need additional people to help you? Do you need money? Education? Equipment? If you do, then you have to work them into your schedule. Utilize the strengths and talents of other people to help you. Most successful people are experts at bringing together the great talent that is available to help them achieve their goals. Coordinate your efforts.

9. **Tell Everyone**. Do not keep your goals a secret. Involve your family and friends. It is much harder to back out and give up on your goals when you create accountability by tell-

ing others. They can provide support by encouraging you. If you fail to involve them then they may not understand why sacrifices need to be made, and they may become a roadblock. Take the time to include everyone and seek their help, advice, and ideas to increase your chances for success. Also, realize that they may not support your goals. They may think you have lost your mind. Do not allow them to discourage you.

10. **Keep Goals Visible**. Place your goals where you are sure to see them. The more often you see them, the better chance you have of staying focused on them. Find pictures that represent them if you need another reminder.

11. **Be Patient**. Not everything will change overnight for you. Success takes time. Most people give up when the changes they want to happen do not happen quickly enough. Doing a little bit every day helps you reach your goals.

12. **Temporary Failure**. You will experience temporary failure. No matter how good you are at planning, things do not always go accordingly. Be flexible and be willing to adjust your plan. Your strong mindset helps you overcome temporary failure and gets you back on track.

13. **Reward Yourself**. Take the time to reward yourself and everyone who has helped you as you reach milestones on your way to the end goal. Rewards keep you motivated. Your reward can be anything that motivates you.

14. **Never Give Up**. If you quit, you lose. There is no future if you quit.

Now that you know what is required for each goal, the next step is to break down your goals into smaller goals. Break them down to the point where you have the smallest daily steps. When scheduling your daily activities determine the best time of day to do each activity.

Write the activities and steps in your new **Daily Log** to show you what you are going to accomplish in each block of time.

For example, if one of your goals is to write a book, at first that goal might seem impossible. If you break it down into writing one page per writing day it seems very possible. If you block the timeslot of 9 p.m. to 10 p.m. Monday, Tuesday, and Thursday to do nothing but write your one page, then you have broken it down to the daily step you need to take.

If you are looking for a job, the first step is to write your resume. Show what you are capable of doing as well as what you have done. Find the places where you want to work and research them. Learn as much as you can about them. Then tailor your resume for each place and go see them day after day. Not just one day. Keep going back. Maybe someone quit, retired or got fired the day after you dropped by. Show them you want to work there. Work for free for 30 days, if that is what it will take to prove your worth.

What if your goal is to repair a broken friendship? The first step is to determine what caused the problem in the friendship. Determine if you are part of the problem, and accept part or all of the blame. Contact the friend and let them know what the relationship means to you, that you are to blame or partly to blame and why you feel that way. If they are not interested in the friendship anymore, move on. Let them know the door is always open if they change their mind.

By breaking down your long-term goals into smaller goals and steps, it makes the goals much easier to achieve. Taking one step at a time simplifies the whole process. Focus on the activities right in front of you and avoid looking too far off into the future. Break down the impossible goal into possible steps, and only focus on one step at a time. That is how the impossible becomes the possible.

You have to measure your progress. If you stray from your plan then you have to make adjustments to get back on schedule. Determine if the plan is the problem or if you are the problem. Something needs to change in order to get you back on track, and most of the time you need to change, not the plan or goals. If your goals are easily achieved, then you must adjust your daily goals and plan to do more. Get tough on yourself!

The following tips are for managing each day to achieve the most success.

1. **Determine** what needs to be accomplished each day. This is your plan. Your plan lists the actions you must take. Write it in your **Daily Log** the night before so you are ready.

2. **Wake up Early** each day. Your competition is up early.

3. **Health.** Your health is your most important priority. Take care of it and it takes care of you. Let it go to waste and you go to waste. Mental and physical exercise, diet, proper sleep, and laughter should all be part of your daily plan. Breakfast is the most important meal of the day, so start your day with a healthy breakfast. Eat healthier meals. Do not deny yourself your favorite foods, even if they are not the healthiest for you, but choose a healthier menu overall. Drink plenty of water to keep your body hydrated and cleansed.

4. **Make Decisions**. Indecision stops progress.

5. **Take Action**. Action gets results.

6. **Stay Focused**. You can only achieve what you focus on.

7. **Stay Disciplined**. Continue to go after what you want every day.

8. **Be Enthusiastic**. Enjoy what you are doing.

9. **Analyze Your day**. At the end of each day (middle of the day also), analyze your progress. Accountability is a key to success. Goals have no meaning unless you hold yourself accountable. Did you hit your goals? You have to know where you are, where you are going, and how you are going to get there. It is like being lost in your car. If you cannot figure out where you are, then you do not know which way to go. At the

end of each day plan your next day, so there is no guesswork as to what you are going to do. If you plan it then you do not have to think about it, you just do it.

10. **Revise your plan.** There is usually a gap between where you are and where you want to be. Adjust your plan, if necessary, to fill the gap. Evaluate the effectiveness of your actions towards achieving your goals and determine if they need adjusting. You also have to be able to plan for anything that might happen because of your actions. Know the possible outcomes for each of your actions, so you are ready with solutions for any problems that arise. Cover your bases.

11. **Bedtime.** Are you visualizing your next day? Make sure you read the list of **Success Thoughts.**

The challenge for most people is that they do not pay attention to what they are doing. The closer you pay attention to the details, the more accurate your plan is. Do the right job, and do the job right.

Live your life in such a powerful way that the day-to-day actions you take send a great message to the world about who you are and what you are up to!

Be An Action Hero

Taking Action is the difference between success and failure. Be a person of action. Most people react instead of act. They wait for something to happen and then react to it. You cannot wait. You have to make things happen. You have to be the action hero. In every action movie, someone steps forward and takes action to conquer the problem, while everyone else runs and hides. Movies imitate life. Action separates you from the competition. It is the only way to be successful. Have you ever stood on the high diving platform and looked over the edge? Many people look over the edge and stop. They go right up to the edge, but never take action. They stop right at the edge of success. You have to **do** something in order to **get** something. If you do nothing, then you get nothing.

Taking action increases your self-confidence and self-worth and crushes the fear that causes most people to freeze up and move away from whatever is causing the fear. Fear limits action. Successful people have fear, but they push past it. The success journey begins with the action of taking a single step. The first step is crucial. Most people never take that first step.

When you literally get hungry, what do you do? You take action to find something to eat. Nothing else gets in your way. You stop doing whatever else you were doing and focus on finding something to eat. You want to get hungry for your dreams so that you take action. Hunger demands that you take action to feed your hunger! Most people do not succeed due to a lack of hunger. Successful people are simply hungrier than everyone else.

You have to act like the person you want to be. Most people say one thing, but believe and do another. Your actions reveal your true belief and the real you. Instead of simply thinking about your beliefs, you have to live them. Be them. Do not think of being a great person, be one. You are your behavior. If you want to be a writer be one. You are one as of now. Believe it. Start writing. If you want to be a singer or musician then get busy writing, recording and selling your songs on the internet and everywhere you can think of. If you want to start a business, then as of now you are a business owner, so get started. Take that first step. Start writing your business plan right now! If you want to be a great salesperson, you are one now, from this moment forward! If you think you are a great person, but act differently, then you are not a great person. If you tell people you are a positive person, but you complain all the time, then you are not a positive person. How many people claim to be religious, but sin, sin, sin? They are not living as they claim. Be an example to people. Do not be a warning of what not to do. What you say means nothing. What you do means everything. Be a great person. Be a great spouse, mate, friend, parent, coworker, student, businessperson, volunteer, etc. Act like the person you want to be.

Neglecting to do what you need to do on a daily basis is a guarantee for failure, leading to lost opportunities, lost income, lost freedom, etc. Remember, you are one step, one phone call, one meeting, or one contact away from huge success. Take action now!

Managing Lean

Managing lean means eliminating waste and continually challenging the way you spend your time. Continue making improvements. Just because you are experiencing success does not mean you are doing everything right. Success can make you lazy. It can make you think that achieving it is easy. Your competition is always right behind you and closing in fast. Continuous success requires continuous improvement. Make sure you optimize your step-by-step processes for success. The first time you develop a step-by-step process it usually contains wasted steps. Lean it out. Eliminate repeated steps or combine several steps into one step. Improve the quality of your work so you do not have to do things over. Each step has to add value to the process. Shorten the time spans for accomplishing each step. Be committed to continuous improvement in everything you do. Think lean! Get lean!

Stress Kills - Managing Stress

A huge factor in determining your long-term health is how you deal with stress. Stress will kill you. You do not even know the constant stress you are under until it is too late. Since the mind and body work as one system, stress is always influencing your entire body. It is a main cause of such health-related issues as depression, cancer, dementia, anxiety, etc. You name the illness and it can be a factor. It is a major reason people fail to take action. It can immobilize you if you cannot find a way to deal with it. It can cause you to lose interest in your dreams. It saps the energy right out of you. The ability to understand and observe what is happening in your life at all times is a big key to managing your stress and achieving success.

Dealing With Stress

You want to eliminate as much stress as you can by reducing the causes. For the stress that you cannot eliminate, you need to increase your tolerance for it. Many people resort to excessive use of alcohol and drugs to deal with their stress, but your mind and body are much more powerful weapons to use. Use the following methods for dealing with stress.

1. **Put Limits** on your hours. Give yourself a break once in awhile.
2. **Isolation.** Isolate the problem causing the stress. If it is something within your control then search for solutions. If it is out of your control then work around it. Accept what you can control, and accept what you cannot control.
3. **Healthy Living.** Sleep, relaxation, and diet are extremely important to your health and stress levels. You want to prevent stress and illness from showing up in the first place. Lack of sleep increases your stress. Many people turn to poor eating habits. Resist these bad habits by doing just the opposite.
4. **Exercise** is the best stress reducer, but unfortunately, most people avoid it. Physical exercise positively impacts your mental state more than you might think, because the mind and body are one system. The better you feel physically, the better you feel mentally. Plan your physical health as well as your mental health. Find a way to incorporate physical exercise at least 3 times per week. This does not mean spending 3 hours a day in the gym. Brisk walking for 20-30 minutes a day does

wonders for your stress levels. Do not forget to stretch, stretch, stretch. Stretching is a great stress reliever. Do whatever exercising you can, but you must do something. The first thing most people do when they arrive home from work is sit down and turn on the television. Rather than taking a seat, take a brisk walk. You can walk or run in place if the weather prevents it. If you absolutely have to watch your favorite television program, then exercise while you are watching. Even if you are sitting down you can still exercise. There are no excuses. If you are in better shape, then your body requires less sleep. You think more creatively. You possess higher levels of energy. You can handle more stress. You can handle more rejection. You feel better and have more confidence. At any point in your day, if you ever need instant energy, simply sit up straight in your chair or stand up and take a few deep breaths. Stand/sit tall, throw in a smile and a laugh, and it instantly changes your energy level.

5. **Relaxing/Quiet Time.** Spend some part of your day in total silence or outside listening to the birds, breeze, etc. Avoid noise. Some people might consider birds to be noise. Use calming music, scents, and certain activities/hobbies that help you relax by disengaging your mind from all your stress-causing worries. Try slow, deep breathing to help you relax. Close your eyes and focus on your breathing. Five minutes each day does wonders for you. Some people like to meditate. Try it. Do whatever works for you.

6. **Volunteer** your time to better someone else's life. Helping others, especially the less fortunate, will give you more satisfaction and happiness than any monetary success. Teach them what you know. Find a way to contribute! Give back.

7. **Educate** yourself so that you are better prepared to deal with everything that comes your way. Read as much as you can on topics of your choice.

8. **Humor** is very healthy for you. It feels great to laugh. Enjoy yourself. Lighten up and have a good time.//
9. **The Positive View.** Look at all the things that are right in your life. Focus on the positives instead of the negatives.
10. **Now Thinking.** Focus on **now**, not yesterday or tomorrow.
11. **Practice.** Is your stress level elevated during certain activities? If possible, practice the stress-causing activities to bring normalcy to that activity. For example, if you have to give a speech every month that causes you stress, find an outlet for speaking four times each month, so speaking becomes more natural to you.
12. **Rewards.** Once again, reward yourself. Do not wait for a rare occasion to celebrate. Simply being alive every day is enough to celebrate! Do not wait for tomorrow!

Do not let stress stop your progress. Know that it is always present and deal with it before it deals with you.

Managing Your Environment

Your environment must support your goals. It impacts you by either building you up or tearing you down. You must be in charge of your own environment so you reduce the risk of becoming a victim of it.

Physical Environment: Your home, place of employment, furniture, equipment, computer, etc., factor into your success. Does your physical environment support your success or not?

People Environment: The people in your life help determine your success. You have to be associated with people who support you. Hang out with the right people, not the wrong people. Hang out with winners and you have a better chance of becoming a winner. Find people who take action. Stay clear of negative and jealous people who badmouth everyone more successful than them. They might think people became successful by cheating or getting lucky. They do not realize what it takes to be successful. Help them change.

Community: Build a sense of community with the people around you. Community is something very much in need. Be the one to start it in your community. Meet your neighbors. Start an exercise program by organizing a weekly walk. Help your neighbors. Give back.

Take a good look at your environment and determine if you need to make changes. Create **your** great environment.

Leverage With Assistants And Outsourcing

People are the most powerful form of leverage you can use. Henry Ford was a master at bringing together the people required to get the job done. He did not build his empire all by himself.

Start building your organization by hiring an assistant and delegate your personal and/or professional activities to them. This is called **leverage**. Have them run errands, answer phones, coordinate appointments, handle administrative duties, solve problems, brainstorm ideas, build and work with your website, marketing, etc. It is time to get help when you do not have time to get everything done. You not only have to hire them but you have to train them. Training them is easy if you have step-by-step processes for your business. They should be able to look at your processes and do the job. Teach them well and challenge them to learn and grow. Work with them to set their goals. Their goals should contribute to your goals. Pay them well, so you keep them as long as possible. Pay them at the level you expect them to perform at and hold them accountable to perform at that level. You get what you pay for, so hire a great person, not a good person.

Outsourcing allows you to hire other professionals who are faster and more cost-effective than you are at doing certain tasks. It is no different than hiring someone to paint your house, install your roof, or fix your car. Hire them so you can focus on doing what you need to be doing. Find experts outside of your expertise and hire them.

Leadership – Managing People

You are at the helm of the ship. You are conducting the orchestra. Provide a feeling of security and support for the people working for you. They want to work in a safe environment that allows them to do their best work. People work best when they enjoy their job and the people they are working with. They do not want to be looking over their shoulder fearing the wrath of someone. Provide a great environment because success is a collaborative undertaking. They will do their part if you provide them with what they need. Leaders have to be problem solvers. Everyone is counting on you to make the right decisions.

Some leaders do not respect the people they work with. You have to like and respect people. Your people are your most important asset so treat them that way. Support them. You are nothing without them. Do not take the attitude that they are nothing without you. If you work well with your group then things go much more smoothly. Make your company a comfortable place for everyone to do their part. If you are uptight they are going to be uptight. If you can put everyone at ease your chances of success increase. You are the one at the top so you have to be the most positive and trustworthy person in the company. If your company is a failure it is your fault. If your company is a success it is because of everyone else. Do not be afraid to take the blame and to give out the credit. You will go far knowing and implementing those two things.

Be confident in your decision-making. Be secure enough to allow everyone to provide his or her input. Their input is gold! Involve them. Work with them to better your company. Ruling with an iron fist and a closed mind causes problems. **Rule number one** is never yell at anyone. You are the leader. Lead by example. Even if they are yelling at you, you have to keep a cool head. Once your voice is raised in anger it is no longer a discussion, it is an argument. Nobody wins an argument. You are in charge. Act like it. **Rule number two** is praise people in public and discipline in private. Give all the praise to everyone else. If you have to discipline someone then do it in private. No one likes to be put on the spot or embarrassed in front of others. Take them aside if you need to, but always show respect for people. If you made the decision to hire them, then accept the blame if they do not perform up to your standards. Either work with them or find their replacement. That is your responsibility.

You have to lead and trust people to do their part. Leadership centers on relationships and communication. If you are not speaking the same language there will be problems. You have to deal with many things going on all at once. You have to be able to make decisions. If you are tentative, people will take advantage of your lack of decision-making. Your job is to make sure everyone has what he or she needs to do his or her job. You have to ensure everything is in place when it needs to be.

Managing Your Database

In order to be successful you have to involve other people. Everyone you meet is important. From a janitor to a CEO, treat them all the same. Build a database full of people that can help you in your success. Your daily goal is to add new contacts to your database. They might be people you must meet who are important contacts in your areas of interest, or future customers/clients. Treat everyone as a lifelong friend. Cultivate relationships for referrals and repeat business.

Managing your database is one of the single most important aspects of long-term success. Communicate with your database by calling, emailing, texting, blogging, holding seminars and webinars, sending newsletters and handwritten letters, having lunch, dinner and outings, or whatever the new method for contact is at the time.

Determine how often to contact him or her and set up a schedule for every person. It all comes down to understanding people's needs and filling those needs.

Building your database and building relationships with your database are important to your success. A big database leads to big opportunities! Go Big!

Managing Your Finances

"The rich always get richer." "It takes money to make money." Those two sayings are very true, but they also leave out one important thing. Anyone can obtain wealth by managing his or her finances. The majority of millionaires in the world did not become millionaires by making great sums of money. They became millionaires by not spending great sums of money. They do not buy material things until they can actually afford them. Can you live without something? If so, then live without it. Keeping track of your money flow is an important part of managing your life. The best way to stay poor is to spend more than you make. You have to think long term instead of looking for the short-term satisfaction you get from buying things. I want you to be able to afford whatever you want once you are in a position to pay for it. Most people spend everything they earn no matter how much they earn. When they make more, they spend more. Keep track of what you do with your money. As a rule, you need to save at least 10% to 15% of your income every week. Some sacrifice is required to save and invest your money, but in the end, you will come out ahead of everyone who did not or could not make the sacrifice. Success requires sacrifice.

Justify all expenses. Determine if the expenses are necessary. Always track your money. You work hard to make money, so you should work twice as hard to keep it. Make your money work for you by investing it. Every dollar you invest must increase income or reduce expenses.

1. **Income**. How do you make your money? How would you like to make your money? If you are planning to start a business, you must determine how much you can afford to lose on that business. At some point, you will only want to spend more money if you are sure of making money. You cannot keep pouring money into something that is not going to pan out. Be realistic about the possibility of success.

2. **Return On Investment (ROI)**. Hold yourself accountable for your money results. Do not let your spending/costs increase without an increase in your results. Re-evaluate expenses all the time. Have goals for your investments and measure the actual results. Know the gap between the two. The actual numbers show you the direction you are heading.

3. **Stick to the Budget**. Always follow your budget.

4. **Expenses**. Keep your personal and professional expenses as low as possible for all areas.

5. **Credit Cards**. The number one problem when it comes to managing personal finances is credit cards. Use them sparingly and be able to pay them off each time you use them. Never pay just the minimum payment each month. Manage your card balances until you can pay them off. If you have a card offering zero interest on balance transfers then take advantage of them, but watch out for the balance transfer fees. Once that zero interest time limit is over, you have to pay it off or shift that money to another card. Keep working on your debt to eliminate it.

6. **Protecting Your Assets**. You must protect your money. Just as you cannot let someone else determine your future, you cannot let someone else protect your money. Friends steal from each other. Family members steal from each other. You cannot trust anyone with your money. If an investment oppor-

tunity seems too good to be true, then run away from it. Educate yourself in order to invest your money wisely.

7. **Streams Of Income**. Have you ever heard of this term? It simply means using leverage to earn money, without having to trade your time to earn the money. At a job you are trading your time for money. You get paid for being at the job. Find a way to make money without having to be present at a job. Investments and rental real estate are ways to leverage your money. Start a business on the internet. You can develop a huge customer base and sales force by using the internet. Develop products that continue to sell without you having to put more energy into them. The best position to be in, is when you leverage your money into producing income without you working.

8. **Taxes**. Prepare your own taxes. You will learn how the tax system works and you will learn the rules of business. Do it!

Conclusion

There is an old saying about the road being paved with good intentions. People make promises with the best intentions of keeping them, but something always gets in the way. There will always be something else going on in your life to take your time away.

You have to maximize the return on your time by managing every area of your life. Everyone has 24 hours each day. What are you going to do with your 24 hours? What is the most valuable use of your time? You have to do the most important things each day. You have to focus on the activities that bring you the most success. Work smarter. If you manage your life, you can accomplish whatever you want. It is all up to you!

3
Success Marketing

"The world is waiting for your arrival"

Welcome to the Marketing Material. You are probably wondering why marketing? The reason is simple. It is all marketing! Marketing touches every aspect of your life. Everything you see, do, eat, wear, etc., is marketed. In the world, there is just one, big, massive, global market. It surrounds you. For you to turn your dreams into reality you have to utilize marketing. The more you know about it the better your chances for success. Just remember, it is all marketing!

You might think of marketing as selling only a product, service or idea, but your skills are a product as well. If you are trying to find a job, you are marketing your skills to prospective employers. If you are already working then you are marketing your accomplishments as an employee in order to keep your job, get promoted and/or receive an increase in pay. If you are trying to meet someone special to develop a personal relationship, then you are marketing your qualities as a good mate. If someone is interested in you, then he or she is marketing his or her qualities to you and you are on the receiving end of that marketing. I do not want you to think of yourself as a product, because you are so much more than that, but you must market your skills and qualities.

For the rest of the marketing part of this book, the word "product" represents your skills, products, services and ideas.

There is only one rule of marketing. If you would not sell your product to your own family, then you should not be selling it to anyone. It is not about manipulating someone to make a quick dollar. It must be a benefit to everyone involved. Every action you take causes a reaction somewhere, so make sure the reaction is positive.

Marketing is a mixture of art and science. The subjective nature of marketing will have you smiling one minute and banging your head against a wall the next. Some strategies work on some people in some areas and then do not work on others in other areas. You have to deploy different strategies and make changes to those strategies on a consistent basis to keep them working. The changes are often small changes rather than major changes. Even if a strategy is working, it can always be improved.

Every marketing piece you put out into the world must show the benefits of doing business with you. You must show potential customers why they should choose your product over the competition. You have to build a great reputation and awareness in the market to earn the trust of potential customers.

Marketing is a daily activity. You never know when something big is going to happen so market, market, market!

Product Life Cycle

Products go through a life cycle made up of four phases or stages: Introduction; Growth; Mature; Decline. You must understand what phase/stage the market is in. If you are just entering the market with a product you must know where the life cycle is for that type of product. Are you creating a brand new market with a brand new type of product never before seen or are you entering a market that already exists and trying to gain market share from the existing competitors? Know where to position your product based on the current product life cycle.

Marketing Plan

Every product starts with an idea in someone's mind and then proceeds to development of the product to be marketed. Most people do not see all the market research that goes into determining what to develop and when, how to develop it, produce it, price it, package it, promote it, deliver it, support it, and keep customers coming back for more.

Once you have a product in mind then you need to start with a marketing plan. Oh no, not another plan! Yes, another plan! Even if you are job hunting, you still need a plan. A marketing plan starts with defining who you are and what your goals are, no matter whether you are an individual or a company. Then you perform a situational analysis of the market, covering all possible impacts that help you determine how to position your products in the market. Once you have that analysis you can develop the strategies you will use to market your products.

The following outline shows the different sections of a marketing plan.

1. **Executive Summary/Marketing Vision.** This is an overall summary of your marketing plan. It includes the major high-level goals, such as globally being number one in your industry or the entertainer of the year or the perfect fit for a job opening. Who are you, and what is your purpose? Are you an individual, a small company or a huge global corporation? What is the vision you have? Is it to find a job? Maybe your corporation's plan is to rule the world.

2. **Objectives.** Your objectives are more-detailed goals for your marketing that need to be measured. What is your product? What is the market for your product? What are your sales objectives? Maybe one objective is to sell $100 million of your product to the under-25 age group by July of next year or own 20% of the over-65 market. These objectives do not cover

budgets, product pricing, etc., which are determined as part of the marketing strategies used to achieve the objectives.

3. **Situation Analysis.** This is where marketing research is performed to collect information and evaluate the current market situation and trends in your market, to determine your potential customers and competitors.

   a. **Company Analysis.** Provide the details about your company. Provide details about the expertise, skills and experience of your company and the people in your company. What is the financial health of your company? If you were looking for a job then your personal expertise, skills and experience would be what you would provide in this analysis.

   b. **SWOT Analysis.** SWOT stands for Strengths, Weaknesses, Opportunities and Threats. It is used to analyze your company and your competition to determine your market. Strengths and weaknesses are internal to you or your company, and opportunities and threats are external to you or your company. What are your strengths that give you an advantage over your competition? What are your weaknesses that put you at a disadvantage when compared to your competition? What are your opportunities in the market? What are the threats to you and/or your business?

   c. **Customer Analysis.** You need to analyze the billions of people that inhabit the earth and determine which ones are your potential customers. Who is your ideal customer? What are they buying and why? What do you know about them? What is their age, gender, income, location, need, etc., that identifies them? You must determine why you are targeting a certain market. What solution are you providing them? What are the benefits they receive from your products? How big is your market and what phase is it in? Once you have determined who is in your market then you can further break down your market into groups or segments and describe each segment. Each piece of your marketing may be different for the different segments that make up your market. For example, if you have a product for the 25-65 year-old market. Maybe you want to market to the 25-35 year-old segment differently than the 36-50 year-old segment and the 51-65 year-old segment. If you are job hunting, make a list of all the companies you are interested in and then break it up into segments. Who are they hiring, and why? What skills and experience are required? Each company segment may have different needs than the others so you would want to tailor your resume to each segment. You might only market to certain segments of your market rather than all of them.

d. **Competitor Analysis.** Who are your competitors, and what is their market share? Include them in your SWOT. Study your competition. What marketing strategies do they use to promote and sell their products? How do they persuade their customers? What is their price? Do they offer discounts all year, only at certain times of the year, or never? Do they offer discounts for multiple-quantity buys? What is their return and cancellation policy? How do they distribute their product? How do they retain customers once they buy?

e. **Collaborators.** Who can you work with to develop and sell your products?

- Subsidiaries
- Distributors
- Venture Capitalists/Angel Investors

- Joint Ventures (JV)
- Affiliates
- Celebrities/Event Sponsorship

f. **Climate.** How do the following factors impact your current and future markets, especially your costs and product pricing? If you are hunting for a job, how do these factors impact the job market?

- Government. How do the local, state, federal and foreign governments impact your market? Do they control the economy in which you do business? Some factors include areas such as investment and economic policy, health policy, education, stimulus, tax policy, environmental policy, regulation, trade and tariffs, etc.
- Legal. Legal issues can have a huge impact on your business. Different areas of law covering health, family, discrimination, employment, anti-trust, safety, technology, etc.
- Technological. Technology impacts your company, especially if you are in the electronics or computer industries. Change is rapid and constant. Look at the huge impacts from the internet, digital and mobile platforms.
- Economic. Factors include the cost to borrow (interest rates), exchange rates (outsourcing and import/export), growth of the economy, inflationary/recessionary climate, etc.
- Ecological/Environmental. Businesses related to farming, logging, fishing, construction/development, tourism, insurance, food processing, grocery, etc.

- Social and Cultural. Trends, health consciousness, population growth rate, age distribution, etc. The new social media has had a huge impact on many industries and how they market using this channel.

- Military/Civil Unrest. Instability in your markets can have a huge impact on your business.

4. **Marketing Strategies.** Once you know your market segment, you must develop the strategies you will use to achieve your goals. These strategies are referred to as the Marketing Mix. The marketing mix used to be known as the classic 4 P's: product, price, place and promotion. Now the mix can have up to 10 P's and more. Create your own mix. List all of the strategies you can think of. Keep track of the ones you use as well as the ones you do not use. You may need to fall back on some of the non-used strategies as the market changes.

   a. **Product.** Consists of the products you are marketing. What are the advantages of your products and how will they be used to market to your customers. Product decisions should include:

   - Brand Name if you have one. This includes the message and look of your brand. Your brand has to show value and why customers buy it over the competition. People should know your brand when they see it.

   - Quality. Is your product the highest quality on the market, the lowest, or in between? Normally, the higher the quality the higher the development and production costs, which lead to a higher sales price.

   - Product Line. Do you have more than one product? Do you have an entire product line?

   - Warranty. Do you offer a warranty? What are the details of that warranty?

- Packaging. How is the product packaging/presentation designed to increase sales? Sometimes packaging is broken out as another P in the marketing mix.

b. **Price.** The prices of your products are determined by many always-changing factors such as supply and demand, cost to produce the product, break-even analysis, competition, perceived value of your brand and what customers are willing to pay. Pricing decisions include:

- List price
- Discounts. Do you offer student and teacher discounts, early matinee discounts, multiple quantity-buy discounts, etc.?
- Rebates/Coupons
- Product Bundling. Do you bundle your products with other products in your line or other companies' products?
- Pricing terms such as fixed price, cost-plus, time plus material, etc.
- Financing options. Do you provide financing for customers?
- Leasing

c. **Place** (Distribution). How will you distribute your products? Where are your products produced, stored and delivered? Decision variables include:

- Distribution channels such as direct sales, wholesale/retail, distributors, mobile, internet, bundling with other products, etc.
- Logistics include transportation, warehousing and order fulfillment.

d. **Promotion.** How will you promote your product to your market? Do you have a message/slogan describing who you are and what you provide? What is your budget for promoting each product in each of your markets? How will you use the different avenues of promotion, such as the internet, email, fax, search engine (optimization), TV, radio, billboards, movies, speaking, print (magazine, newspaper, direct mail), mobile, social media, product placement, viral, keyword ads, trade shows, giveaways/samples, lunch-n-learns, article-writing, blogs, sponsorship (teams, groups, schools, causes, events, donations/charities, community service), referrals, promotional items with your logo (t-shirts, coffee cups, pencils, pens, bumper stickers, mouse pads, etc.)? You must be creative enough to set yourself apart from your competition. You must track your promotions to determine which ones are working. See the material below on **Writing Advertisement Copy** for tips on how to write your ads.

e. **Physical.** What does the customer actually see, taste, experience, etc., before making their buying decision? Most products can be seen in person. The auto industry shows their new models at auto shows and then in their showrooms and on their lots. You can test drive them. Clothing can be tried-on to see how it looks and fits. The movie industry releases a trailer of the movie. The music industry plays their music on the radio, internet, etc. The food and beverage industry often provides free samples for tasting. The service industry uses referrals and testimonials from past customers.

f. **People.** Who are the people representing your business and who are the customers buying your product?

g. **Process.** What is the process your customers go through to learn about and buy your product? It starts with the first contact they have with you and your product and the process never ends, because of your long-term customer relationship building.

    h. **Timing.** When is the best time to implement each strategy? Schedule your implementation. Timing is everything.

5. **Marketing Material.** Everything you use to market your products such as samples, brochures, websites, articles, newsletters, professional white papers, etc., fall under marketing material. Your material must promote your brand and identify the benefit you provide to your customers.

6. **Sales Management.** Do you have a sales force? Do you have a sales plan? Your sales force may be the only communication you have with your customers. Treat your sales force well and give them the training, tools and resources to be successful in generating revenue. Motivate them by providing them with residual commissions/bonuses for repeat sales to customers; otherwise they lose interest in building relationships with their customers and will only focus on finding new customers.

7. **Lead Conversion and Retention Plan.** How do you convert your leads once you have them? What is your sales strategy and Customer Relationship Management (CRM) Plan? How will you keep your customers once they buy? You must support your products after they are sold to your customers and build loyalty for future business. Get feedback from your customers. They will give you the answers you need to keep them as a customer. Once you have a customer you never want to lose them to your competition.

8. **Execution/Action plan.** The steps/actions you need to take to execute your plan.

9. **Projections.** Project your gross and net revenue over the short term and long term. Use actual revenue, if you have any, for your future projections.

10. **Conclusion.** A summary of all of the above

    a. **Appendix.** Include product brochures, product specs, etc.

    b. **Exhibits.** Include advertising samples, promotions, product samples (images), charts, graphs, and calculations of market size, commissions, profit margins, break-even analysis, etc.

The Test Market

Before you spend a ton of money putting yourself and/or your product out into your target market, test the market. Ask people for their opinion of your product and their ideas for improvement. If you are job hunting, have someone review your resume and give you a mock interview. Most filmmakers run test screenings of their films and ask the audience for feedback. Some market research companies specialize in providing test markets for other companies' products. You can participate in test markets/focus groups for products and experience how to run your own test market/focus group for your products. Search for them. They are always looking for people to test products, and often times you will be paid as well as receive free products.

Press

This is an attention economy, meaning those who get the most attention have the best chance for success. One of the most important marketing strategies you can create is your own press. Press is something that is relatively inexpensive for you to develop and allows you to create a buzz for you and your products.

Timing is important. Be ready when the time comes to hit the press. Get yourself in the industry news. Use your skills/experience for speaking events and seminars, and do interviews for radio, TV, newspapers, websites, magazines, etc. Give free advice and build your credibility. Make them aware of your unique products or expertise. You must tell them why your story is worthy. Some controversy can be good. Give them a story they cannot refuse.

Submit a Press Kit and promotional items to all possible outlets for interviews, and then call them. Your press kit needs to include the following items and anything more you feel might peak their attention.

1. **Synopsis** of you and your products/business. One page or shorter in length.

2. **Your Bio**. Include your bio in the kit because you are the focal point. Include your own stories, how you made it happen, hurdles you overcame, etc.

3. **Client & Customer Reviews/Testimonials**. These can be from any source. Ask for reviews/testimonials from clients/customers, newspapers, industry-related magazines, other websites, and respected A-List professionals endorsing you and/or your products. Include copies in your kit, on your website, in your calls, etc.

4. **Publicity Photos**. Photos of you and your products/ business.

5. **Electronic Press Kit** (EPK). An EPK includes everything from above plus audio/video. Put these onto recording media to hand out or send electronically.

Most press kits are electronic and are much cheaper to produce and distribute than the older print version. Send out your press kit anytime you will be doing an interview. Find examples of press kits online. Do not reinvent the wheel; copy the best of the best. Remember, everyday is a day to make something happen. What can you make happen today to get you closer to your goals?

Cross-Platform Marketing

You want to integrate your marketing across traditional media, the internet and mobile.

Traditional Media

Traditional media covers print, radio, TV, billboards, direct mail, etc. Direct mail is not as dead as most people might think. The right campaign will always work if done properly. Postcards are the recommended method because nothing has to be opened, and the information is staring your potential customer in the face the instant they look at the postcard, just like a billboard, TV ad or print ad. You have to grab their attention within 5 seconds. If they have to open a letter then they are already suspicious. They treat it like junk mail. If the letters are hand-written then most people will open them. Provide something of value that they can use.

The Internet

The internet is one of the most promising avenues for marketing. Use your own website as well as email, social media/networking sites, video-posting sites, chat rooms, online groups, etc., to advertise and network, and put yourself and your products out into the world. People spend more time on social media sites than anywhere else online. Make the internet a key part of your marketing strategy.

Mobile Media

Mobile media is fast becoming the preferred choice for digital marketing since more people spend their time glued to their mobile devices. Globally, more people own them than computers or televisions. Purchases using mobile devices are on the rise. Think of mobile as the in-your-pocket internet. Texts and video advertisements sent via mobile are the method for marketing products. Use 15-second long commercials rather than the normal 30-second TV commercials. With mobile marketing, you know exactly who watches your ads. Traditional marketing does not give you that all-important data feedback. Make mobile marketing part of your marketing mix.

Audio/Video

Marketing yourself and your products through audio/video can be a very powerful strategy. You want to use the old rule of speaking, which is tell them what you are going to tell them, then tell them, and then tell them what you told them. No matter which medium you choose, your target audience is expecting certain things from you.

1. **Emotions**. You must engage people on an emotional level, so they relate to what you are saying or showing. They must identify with the material. Your marketing must speak to them. Use vocabulary that hits at the audience's emotions.
2. **In You They Trust**. Give them the truth.
3. **They Benefit**. It is all about them. Serve them solutions.
4. **Hook Them**. You must hook your audience right from the start. Catch their attention.
5. **Hold Them**. You must hold their attention in this short-attention-span world.
6. **Short and Simple**. Keep your message as short (several minutes) and simple as possible. If you go beyond 5 minutes then you really have to be giving them something great. I am not saying your audio/video cannot be 60 minutes long, but it has to be a worthwhile 60 minutes.
7. **Show and Tell**. Use images, sounds, text, charts, etc., in your video to keep them watching. Mix it up, because each person responds differently to images, text, voice, etc.

8. **Call to Action**. Make sure to close/finish your audio/video with the information and steps they need to take in order to receive additional information or purchase your product. Tell them exactly what they need to do.

Writing Advertisement Copy

Writing good ad copy is key to persuading your customer to buy from you. Use creativity in your message. Use the buzzwords and phrases used by your target customers. Talk their talk. Focus on your customer and give them what they want. Your headline must grab them and persuade them to keep reading and to ultimately buy your products. Each line and word continues to build interest. It is the same as a great film or song. A great film hooks you from the start and keeps you hooked. A great song makes you want to keep listening. It is all about the customer and their desires. Your Principle Selling Position (PSP) or Unique Selling Position (USP) states the benefits of your product and why they should buy from you. It sets you apart from your competition. Connect on an emotional level since emotions are the reason people buy a product. Every company links great feelings to their products, whether it is food and drink, clothing, hair care, make-up, cars, music, film, travel, home furnishings, business ventures, etc. Their marketing shows you how their products benefit you and make your life wonderful. They sell the dream lifestyle. Give the customer what they want. If it is a drink product then it tastes unbelievable and is good for you. If it is a shower gel or soap it leaves you feeling refreshed and clean. Their clothing makes you look good wearing it. Their hair care and beauty products make you smell good and look good, so you can meet the person of your dreams. You will look successful driving their car. You will be entertained listening to their music or watching their film. If they want financial security then your product does that. If they want grass and oil stains washed out of their clothing then your detergent does that. Their products take you from a position of discomfort to a position of comfort. Comfort over discomfort. Pleasure over pain. Heaven over hell. They know how to link their products to your emotions. The emotional attraction to a product makes it so they do not have to sell you anything. You are already sold. The key to great marketing is to show the value customers receive from buying your products. That is selling without selling. Connect with your customer by filling a void they have for love, family, friendship, entertainment, business, security, financial security, physical and mental health, confidence, self-esteem, beauty, acceptance, etc. Marketing sells value. You have to know the value you are selling. What are you solving for your customer? Marketing sells solutions to people's problems. Put urgency in the mind of the customer. If they want to lose weight then your product is the best and fastest product to do that. Car dealers have weekend sales that have a limited number of cars available, so hurry out to buy while the quantities last.

Some ad copy tells the customer what will happen if they do not buy the product. What are the consequences? People often buy on the fear of missing out. People rush out to see a movie the first weekend it opens, so they can talk about it at work on Monday. They do not want to be left out of the conversation.

Provide the action they must take to buy your product and make it urgent. Writing ad copy is selling. You need to understand how to sell. You might not think of yourself as a salesperson, but you are selling all the time. If you convince your family and friends to do something, you are selling. If you smile and say "hello" to someone and they smile or say "hello" back, then you closed the deal and sold them on the smile and greeting. That is persuasion. You involved them in the decision to buy what you were selling. When you realize that both sides need to win then you understand how to sell. You have to earn the right to sell to someone. Set up the deal properly by giving value to people.

Your marketing goal is to reach the point where business comes to you without you having to pursue it, even though you do not want to stop pursuing it. You must continually plant your name, product, brand, etc., in the minds of the potential customers in your target market, so that when they think of whom they want to work with, buy from, associate with and refer, they think of you. You are planting seeds in their mind just as you plant seeds into your own mind.

The rest of the marketing material covers topics related to meeting, working with, persuading, and developing life-long relationships with people. Business has become so impersonal that the best marketing you can do is face-to-face. Get out into the world and shake hands, rub elbows, exchange contact information, make friends, start business relationships, and most important of all, have fun.

People

Your success depends on how well you understand and deal with the different types of people you will meet. The most successful people in the world are the best at understanding, dealing with, and working with people. You cannot treat everyone the same. Everyone is unique with a unique situation. Some people will immediately want to do business with you and some will never want to. Some people will like you and some will not. There are nice people and not-so-nice people. People who tell you what to do and those who ask you what to do. People who can change and those who cannot. Positive people and negative people. Warm and cold. Talkers and action takers. Logical and illogical. Emotional and unemotional. Extroverts, introverts, sensors, influencers, dominators, compliers, thinkers, judgers, feelers, perceivers, helpers, romantics, leaders, followers, enthusiasts, skeptics, etc. Of course you have every mix in between made up of all the possible combinations. The list goes on and on. The point is, when you are dealing with people you have to understand personality types so you treat everyone from a different angle. Learn to read a person's type so you know how to deal with them. This experience can only come from getting out into the market and meeting people.

Perception

The first contact you have with someone is crucial, because people judge you and/or your products within the first few seconds of that initial contact.

What do people think when they first come into contact with you and/or your products? Do they think you are the person they want to hire or work with? Do they feel they can trust you? Do they want to buy your products? The best way to find out is to ask. Do not be shy about asking them for feedback so you can improve.

Make people feel good while they are in your presence. Make them feel important. Be fun and exciting. You want people to feel great when they think of you! All too often you see celebrities, politicians, business leaders, etc., mistreat the very people that support them and allow them to be in the position that they are in. Always make a good impression on people and leave them wanting more of you.

Body Language

Do you pay attention to every little aspect of a person's nonverbal communication? Can you tell when someone is interested or not interested in talking or dealing with you? Can you see the signs? Almost every part of the body provides clues to you as to what they are thinking, feeling, saying, etc. What you think is happening may not be happening at all. You may not be reading their nonverbal signs properly. Nonverbal communication depends on the situation, environment, personality of the other person(s), etc. One type of behavior means one thing in one instance and means something completely different in another instance. You must be able to observe what is actually going on in your communication with people on both a personal and professional level. Educate yourself in body language so you have better success in all of your relationships.

What People Demand

First and foremost you have to be professional. People want to deal with professionals they like and trust. It is an emotional decision as to whether they want to work with you, buy from you and/or refer you. They have to know that you have their best interests in mind. You have to have integrity. Do not compromise it. Once you do, there is no going back. Always be truthful. Being truthful gives you a great feeling inside rather than a guilty and uneasy feeling. You have to be reliable and do what you say you are going to do. Take the extra step. Communicate trust by being there to help them. Always be patient and kind to people. Smile! It is amazing how few people smile. If you manage other people, then teach them these same qualities.

Do these things and separate yourself from your competition. Mistreat people and it comes back to haunt you. Even when you treat people well, some of them will still have a negative view of you, but at least you did your part. The world is a much smaller community than you think, so your reputation is always on the line.

Negotiation

Negotiation is about finding a solution to a situation, problem, deal, etc. The ultimate goal is for both parties to win in the negotiation, but the most important negotiating position you can be in, is when you are willing and able to walk away from the negotiating table without a deal in your hand. You have to be prepared to walk away from the table if you do not get what you need. If you are not in that position then you have a chance of losing in the negotiation. Negotiation is another subject that sends shivers down many spines for the simple reason most people do not do it often enough, and therefore they think they will not get a good deal. If you know your goal before you enter into a negotiation then you should have no fear.

Negotiating is based on a relationship like everything else. Both parties come into a negotiation to win. If you plan on working with these same people or companies again, then treat negotiations as a life-long relationship. Respect the other party, especially if it is a personal matter instead of business. Come into the negotiation with a positive attitude even if the other party does not. They have needs and wants just the same as you do. Even if you cannot come to a deal, always leave the negotiating table on good terms.

Before you start negotiations with anyone, you need to do your homework about them. Do your research to find out as much as you can about how they deal with other people and other companies. Discover their negotiation tactics, so you know what to expect from them and how to negotiate with them. What drives them? Are they driven by integrity? Are they driven by money? Are they driven by desperation? Remember, the material in **The Zone** stated that making a choice under pressure is often not a good choice. Anyone in need is not in a good emotional state to be negotiating.

Know what you want and what you need. Your want is the high end you are shooting for and the need is the bottom line you will take. Let them make the first offer. You want to start with a high offer, so that you can compromise as you come down closer to your goal. If anyone agrees too soon, then maybe they did not ask for enough.

Remember, people buy based on emotions, therefore they often negotiate the same way. You have to keep your emotions in check and take them out of the negotiation. Keep it related to the issues involved. Be objective when negotiating. Base your negotiation on your need and want. The other party may try and persuade you into getting emotional about the deal. Negotiations can often involve some heated discussion, but you must always remain calm. Never get angry or abusive. Do not blame the other party. Keep yourself under control at all times.

Close the deal when you have negotiated what you feel is the best possible deal. Do not waste extra time closing if you have met your goal. You do not want to keep negotiating if it might mean losing the deal. Knowing when to close has to be based on your goal going into the negotiations.

You must also think about your options if you do not reach a deal. How does that impact you and your business? Maybe taking a smaller deal now, might result in larger deals in the future. The real deal is being in a position to walk away from the deal. Only then are you in the right position to negotiate. Know your position and stand your ground.

Schmoozing/Networking

"Oh no, not schmoozing!" That is the scream you will hear from most people. Schmoozing can be fun if you know what to do. Think about the end result. Think of schmoozing as a multi-million dollar activity. Making the right connections can be worth millions to you. That should change your views on schmoozing. Schmoozing represents opportunity. Schmoozing works for every part of your life. Have you ever stood in line at a restaurant, nightclub or event and someone gets escorted right past you? Schmoozers! Who gets the promotions at work? Schmoozers! Who lands the big sales? Schmoozers! Who are the tops in any industry? Schmoozers!

Most people avoid schmoozing because it is a get-out-of-your-comfort-zone activity. Like anything else, once you take action and do that activity it becomes more comfortable to you. Schmoozing is about giving. Schmoozing is about having fun, being nice and enjoying the company of others. Schmoozing is selling without selling. Schmoozing is networking, no matter whether it is in-person, online, on the phone, through traditional marketing, etc. In-person networking is number one. Do not hide behind your desk or computer. Get out into the world. Get out into the market. You have to be in the marketplace to make things happen. The world is out there waiting to meet you, work with you and buy from you. Expand your world by meeting people. Do not sit and wait for the phone to ring like most people. Make your phone ring. You have to be the type of person who makes things happen. Take action and people will be calling you, because they need what you have to offer.

You have to pick the right people to schmooze. Find your target market. If you know in advance with whom you will be meeting, do your research about them and their company so you have things in common to talk about. It shows your interest since you took the time to research them. Often times people only want to schmooze the top people, but strike up a conversation with anyone you can, because you never know who may be running the show one day.

Show up early to meetings, whether you are meeting with an individual, group or company. When attending large events, showing up early gives you the advantage of seeing everyone arrive. If you show up late then you have to play catch-up. Fashionably late is not in fashion. You do not want to show up late and find everyone already engaged in group discussions. If you said you were going to show up and then decide not to, then you have to let people know. Emergencies are the only possible excuse. Nobody wants to work with undependable and unprofessional people.

Walk into and out of a room in a positive manner no matter what happens. Schmoozing can be a nerve-wracking experience, even if you know everyone who will be attending, because the end result may be more rejection. As soon as you approach someone you can tell whether they are welcoming you or hoping your stay is a short one. Fear of rejection is the main reason people do not show up even when they say they will.

Making small talk is important. Be prepared to start conversations instead of relying on others. If you have several prepared conversation starters you can walk up to a complete stranger and start a conversation. Those that have a difficult time starting a conversation are usually the ones who fear schmoozing the most. They will usually walk up to a group and try to get involved. It is best to walk up to someone standing alone and make conversation rather than jumping into another group. He or she will usually welcome your company. Of course, if the person you want to talk to is already within a group then you have no choice but to find a way to get involved in the group conversation. Start with a smile, make eye contact, and introduce yourself. More and more people are not into touching hands these days so a handshake may not be appropriate. If they offer their hand, then by all means shake it.

You want to engage people on their level. If they talk slow and quiet and stand perfectly still then you do not want to talk loud, fast and jump around. Match them, but don't make it obvious.

Listen and ask good questions. The person asking the questions controls the conversation, which is the opposite of what most people think. People love to talk. If you are talking and you see the other person looking everywhere but at you, guess what? You are either talking too much and/or they are not interested. Let them talk. Listen to everything they say. Do not interrupt them. You might learn something. By listening, it allows you to ask more questions in regards to what they are saying. It deepens the conversation and your connection with them.

Say What

Most people do not know what to say to start a conversation. You can start off discussing the setting for the event, but you want to get to the interests and passions of the person you are schmoozing. Keep up on current events and trends in different areas such as news, sports, music, movies, travel, gossip, the economy, etc. Stay on top of what is going on in the world. You want to be able to discuss a variety of topics to find the common ground you have with everyone. Humorous subjects and a fun attitude will win out every time over more serious subjects.

Never bring up topics such as religion, weather, politics or personal problems. Religion and politics are too personal and you never know what might upset a person. You do not want to lose an opportunity because you bashed the political party or religion of the person you are talking to. The weather can be a boring subject. Do not complain or criticize. If you pull out your cell phone during a discussion, you might as well go home, unless there is an emergency. Wait until you are alone to check your text messages, tweets, calls, etc. Get them talking about their personal and professional goals. Find out what they want so you can determine if you can help them.

It can be just as difficult to leave a conversation, as it is to start one. Do not be afraid to leave. The conversation must end at some time and one of you has to end it. Ask for their contact information and make plans to contact them again. Once again, use the setting to get into and out of conversations. You can also go with the old excuse of having to use the restroom, or needing food and a drink if you cannot come up with anything else. If you see someone that you must schmooze, invite the person you are talking to, to come along with you. Always, say hello, good-bye and thank you to the host, and others that you talked to during your time there.

Make sure people can get in touch with you. Exchange email, phone numbers, business cards, etc. Get creative with your business cards by adding an image, story or some kind of message that identifies you and/or your brand. Always carry a card with you no matter where you are going. Give your cards to everyone who is interested in you and/or your products. If someone gives you a business card then offer yours. Build those relationships. Make notes about everyone you meet, so you do not forget his or her information. Determine what went well and what did not. What could you have done differently? Were you in the moment in the room? Were you listening, or were you only trying to talk?

Follow-up within 24 hours. The first follow-up can simply be a "nice-to-meet-you" email, text or letter and mention information about their passions or interests. You want to show them that you are not just sending them another form message. Later follow-ups must add value to the relationship. Do not waste their time. If you continue contacting someone and they do not respond back to you, then wait at least six months before contacting them again. Not all relationships will work so do not push it.

Schmoozing Musts

1. **Show Up as a Professional** in-person and online as well. Do your homework, show up to appointments early, and treat everyone with respect. Look professional for your industry. Create a great impression.

2. **Smile**. It is the first thing to do when approaching someone. It warms people up.

3. **Create Excitement** and enthusiasm. If you have a good time meeting people, then they will have a good time meeting you. Find a sense of humor if you do not have one. You do not have to be a comedian, but be fun, engaging and interesting. Find something to like about everyone.

4. **Firm Handshake**. Give them a firm handshake if they offer their hand first. It is a sign of strength and confidence.

5. **Stay calm**. Be relaxed. Do not take things too seriously. You have to be as comfortable in the presence of your friends as you would in the company of billionaires. People are people.

6. **Learn a Person's Name** and refer to them by their name.

7. **Establish Rapport**. People work with people they like and trust. Be kind and courteous, give a friendly greeting, and show them you care about them. Find out what their expectations are by asking them. Your tone of voice shows your confidence. Pick the right words to use in your communication. Always make other people feel important. Human nature is to want to feel desired and appreciated. To get what you want, you have to give them what they want.

8. **Ask Probing Questions**. Ask easy, open-ended questions that do not have one-word answers. Make sure your questions are positive. Get them talking about themselves and their plans in order to know what you can do for them or if you can do anything for them. You will want to know about

their family, their hobbies and other interests, etc. Obtain their personal information: Birthdays, children, pets, etc. How do you get this information? Do you meet with them in person in their home or office? If so, look around for pictures, awards, diplomas, etc. Don't snoop around. Just pay attention to what they have out in plain view in their home or office.

9. **Focus And Listen**. Look them in the eye when you are talking with them. Successful people listen more than they talk.

10. **The Close**. All of the things you do in your conversation will close the deal. The close is just a formality if you have done everything right from the start.

11. **Follow-up**. The fortune is in the follow-up. Once you have information, you must do something with it. Too many people waste valuable contact information once they get it. Fill your database with the information you gather and put it to good use. Always thank people. Call them. Send cards, personal letters (handwritten "Thank You" notes), email, texts, tweets, etc. Get "face-to-face" with people as much as possible. Use a different holiday besides the usual holidays for sending cards. Think of obscure holidays to peek their interest. The main reason most people do not follow-up is they do not know what to say. If it has been a long time since you contacted someone, apologize for not keeping in touch. People are very busy, so keep it short and add value each time you contact them so they are thankful you did. Contact them at least 4 times per year. Thirty seconds to read your message is all it should take. Make it quick and powerful with words of wisdom or motivation to match their personality and beliefs. Surprise them with a gift. Most people only reward their contacts when they receive something first. A simple gift card means a lot to people. Not communicating with your contacts will mean the end of those relationships.

You cannot afford to lose track of people. The more people you are in contact with the better chance you have for success. Every conversation can result in business.

Where To Schmooze

There are plenty of places to schmooze. Always be ready to talk, because you never know who is standing next to you.

1. **Professional Organizations** Join groups/organizations that support your industry. Many of them are online. Spending time in online forums learning, and sharing your own experience helps you gather valuable information towards achieving your goals. These groups help keep you motivated.

2. **Industry Gatherings** are great places to make contacts. Attend expos, seminars, meet-ups, mixers, panel discussions, etc.

3. **Website/Internet Presence**. Your own website is your electronic business card. Offer a newsletter, articles and/or a "tip of the week" email campaign. This keeps your name in their mind.

4. **Professional Partnering**. You should be pursuing professional partnering opportunities to increase your marketing potential and referral base. See the **Professional Partnering** material for additional information.

5. **Teleseminars/Conference Calls.** Set up and run teleseminars, conference calls and/or webinars in order to provide services, education and business advice to possible clients. Send out a meeting agenda and/or handout prior to the call. Record the calls and use them in your marketing or sell them as a training product.

6. **Dinner for Two**. Dine with clients. Business dining builds strong client relationships. Use other activities like volunteering, sporting events, etc., for schmoozing.

7. **Networking Companies/Small Business**. Offer to come in and present your products to their employees, especially if you offer discounts. Work through their human resources people if they have them. For smaller companies you should go straight to the owner. All you have to do is ask. Ask!

You are in charge of your success. No one else cares about your success as much as you do. You have to be the best promoter of you. People want to work with people who take the initiative. They want movers and shakers. They want to be around people who make things happen. Show them that you are going to be successful and they will want to be a part of it.

Cold Calling

Cold calling is a great way to drum up new business, but it is another fear people have. Cold calling is full of rejection; especially with all the bogus calls people receive. Cold call rejection is usually based on the reason for your call, not you personally, because they do not know you. You have to make your first impression a memorable one. They often decide to work with you based on the first bit of dialogue they have with you. Your calls have to add value to their life. People have their guard up so you have to be ready for that. You have a few seconds to interest them before they hang up. You have to know your market segment so the product you are selling is something they are interested in buying. Some telemarketers give cold callers a bad reputation by trying to sell products to customers who have shown no interest in buying anything. Think like your customer. What would you want to hear from a person cold calling you?

Use a script for your calls. Calling without knowing exactly what you are going to say is a sure-fire way to get rejected. Test and rewrite your script until it sounds natural. As the market changes, change your script. Use the following tips when calling.

1. Smile while talking. It automatically gives you energy and a good feeling to start the conversation.
2. Use a warm sincere voice. It shows a sense of caring on your part.
3. Identify yourself immediately. They want to know with whom they are talking.
4. In one short sentence, state why you are calling. State the benefit to them.
5. If someone referred you, then mention his or her name immediately.
6. Write down all information the customer tells you and repeat it back to them, so you know you have it right.
7. Ask questions to reveal information.
8. In closing, discuss the next step. Discuss the action they must take.
9. Thank people no matter how the conversation goes.
10. If you need to put someone on hold, ask first. Tell them how long they will be on hold.
11. Keep calling. Most cold callers give up on a prospective customer after one call.
12. Use the power words below to influence people.

Words of Influence

The words you use have a big influence on people. The best way to influence them is to make them feel like they are right. The customer is always right. When you agree with people you totally disarm them. They cannot help but like you. Do not tell them they are wrong, even if they are wrong. If they are wrong, slowly work them in your direction. Help them make good decisions that benefit them. Always apologize if an argument ensues.

Here are some phrases to use to win people over.

1. I agree with you.
2. You are absolutely right.
3. No problem.
4. I understand.
5. That is a real concern.
6. Let me make sure I have this right.
7. What I hear you saying is...?
8. What I feel you mean is...?
9. I do not blame you for feeling the way you do. If I were you, I would feel the same way.
10. Allow me.
11. I would be happy to.
12. Would you consider...?
13. How can we work together?
14. Together we can figure it out.

Referrals

Referrals are the goldmine of business. Out of all the marketing you do, referrals are the preferred method to getting business and building your business. If you know a hairdresser who knows the pool-guy who knows the plumber that fixed the leaking shower at the White House then use that line of communication to get to The President. Work any and every contact you have for a referral.

Professional Partnering

Partnering is a great way to develop business. Partner with other professionals and businesses whose strengths are your weakness, as well as others in your industry who are not in direct competition with you. Partnering does not mean you set up a contractual and tax-related partnership. It simply means you are joining forces to increase business for all of you. Look at Joint Ventures and Affiliates below, for two types of partnering.

The more potential partners you communicate with the better chance you will have of finding a few great ones to work with. Partner with as many people as you can handle, but do not stretch yourself too thin. Be very selective of who you get into business with. They do not have to be the top people in your industry, but they have to be like-minded. They have to want to succeed like you.

How do you become the partner they want to work with? It is not as difficult as you think, but it takes work like any other relationship. You want to start your partnership efforts by showing them how they can improve their life and business. The partners interested in working with you know they are working with someone who is going to help them succeed. Teach them to plan, set daily goals, take action, be accountable, etc. Help them grow. This only takes a few minutes each week to coach them. Make them identify their plan for achieving their goals. Everyone can always use a little help and encouragement. Motivate and challenge them.

Joint Ventures

A Joint Venture (JV) is where two or more people or companies work together to improve business. It allows you to expand your market by teaming up with them in the same market segment or other market segments. It allows you to team up in promotional activities that you by yourself may not be able to afford to do. For example, if you own a restaurant and you team up with other restaurants to do a tasting party, or you are a filmmaker and you team up with other filmmakers to show your films at your own film festival. You all have a common goal. You split the marketing costs and hosting duties for that particular event.

Affiliates/Independent Salespeople

Affiliates/independent salespeople sell your products on a commission basis only. They do not receive any other benefits from you or your business. Think of all the market segments for your products and find affiliates in those segments. You can have a huge sales force working for you without having to manage them on a daily basis. Coach and support them to ensure they are properly representing you and your products in the market.

Conclusion

Marketing is a daily activity. Spend time promoting yourself and your products. Implement as many strategies as you can. The more strategies you employ and the wider you go into the world the better chance you have for success.

Find a success recipe that works and keep using it. Get out into the world and network. If you show energy and excitement then it will rub off on others. Target the people you want to be in business with. You have to believe that you are the best at what you do. Believe it and become it!

Learn to adapt to a constantly changing environment. You have to be versatile and flexible. You have to be able to perceive what is actually happening, not what you think is happening.

You cannot hang on to your past. It is long gone. Move forward at all times. You have to be ready when opportunities show up. Be willing to make your own opportunities as well.

Achieve greatness by helping others. Be there to support them when things are not going their way. Teach them how you became successful. The saying goes that smart people learn from their mistakes, but brilliant people learn from other's mistakes. If you can teach others, you will be delivering a great service.

You can make a difference every day. Right now is the time to start! It is all about participation in life! Think big! Take big action! Get ready and fasten your seatbelt, because it is going to be a fun and wild ride. Go for it!

Best wishes for your success,

Curtis Kessinger

P.S. Keep me informed of your success and do not be shy about contacting me to discuss anything you want to discuss.

About the Author

Curtis Kessinger has worked as an independent filmmaker, stand-up comic, improv and voice-over actor, engineer, consultant, tax professional, etc., etc., etc. He continues to chase after whatever dreams he chooses without any regrets. He has worked in the personal coaching business for over ten years and is the founder of Success Minded Coaching. Curtis' education includes: BS in Mechanical Engineering (Southern Illinois University); MBA (Pepperdine University); Filmmaking and screenwriting courses (UCLA & others). He currently lives in the Los Angeles area with his family.

APPENDIX

Daily Log

Daily Log   Day: M T W Th F S S   Month:

Time	
12:30 am	
1:00 am	
1:30 am	
2:00 am	
2:30 am	
3:00 am	
3:30 am	
4:00 am	
4:30 am	
5:00 am	
5:30 am	
6:00 am	
6:30 am	
7:00 am	
7:30 am	
8:00 am	
8:30 am	

9:00 am	
9:30 am	
10:00 am	
10:30 am	
11:00 am	
11:30 am	
12:00 noon	
12:30 pm	
1:00 pm	
1:30 pm	
2:00 pm	
2:30 pm	
3:00 pm	
3:30 pm	
4:00 pm	
4:30 pm	
5:00 pm	
5:30 pm	
6:00 pm	
6:30 pm	
7:00 pm	
7:30 pm	
8:00 pm	
8:30 pm	

9:00 pm	
9:30 pm	
10:00 pm	
10:30 pm	
11:00 pm	
11:30 pm	
12:00 midnight	

Biography Sheet

The Ultimate Question

Why not you?

Family & Friends

1. Your Full Name:
2. Does your name have a special meaning?
3. Do you like your name? Why or why not?
4. What name would you like to have if you could?
5. Birthplace:
6. Where did you grow up?
7. Parents names:
8. Siblings:
9. Relatives:
10. Were you adopted? If so, do you know your biological family?
11. Were you raised in foster care?
12. Who raised you?
13. Who influenced you the most growing up?
14. Was the influence good? Bad? Both? Why?
15. Who means the most to you?

16. Are they still in your life today?
17. Were your parents married? Divorced? Lived together?
18. Are they still together today?
19. Do you remember your childhood home(s)? What do you remember?
20. Experiences as a child: List your good and bad memories.
21. Name your friends and enemies from childhood.
22. Why were they friends or enemies?
23. Do you have many friends? Why or why not?
24. Why are you friends with them?
25. Do you want more friends? Why or why not?
26. Name your favorite and least favorite teachers? Why?
27. Did you play sports? Why or why not?
28. What interests and hobbies did you have?
29. Are you currently in a relationship?
30. If so, what do you like about this person?
31. If so, what do you dislike about this person?
32. How do you think they feel about you?
33. Have you had any bad relationships in the past? Why were they bad?
34. Have you had any great relationships in the past? Why were they great?
35. Describe the best relationship for you?
36. What would you like to change about your relationship(s)?
37. What kind of people do you like to be around? Are you around those types of people? Why or why not?

38. Have you ever been in the military? How did those experiences shape who you are?
39. Do you have or want children? Why or why not?
40. Do you have or want pets? Why or why not?

Education

1. Do you like learning?
2. What subjects are you interested in learning more about?
3. Did you dislike school?
4. If you disliked school was it because you had no interest in the subjects being taught?
5. Would you have done better if you had an interest in the subjects?
6. What level of education do you have?
7. Do you wish you had more education? In what area?
8. Are you currently taking classes? Why or why not?
9. Are you currently learning outside of a classroom setting?

Relaxation/Travel

1. What do you do to relax?
2. Is anything preventing you from relaxing the way you would like?
3. Where do you vacation?
4. Where would you like to vacation?
5. Have you visited other countries? What were your experiences?

6. What countries would you like to visit and why?
7. Is anything preventing you from taking the vacations you would like?

Who, What, When, Where, Why?

1. Who are you?
2. Who are you not?
3. Who do other people think you are?
4. Who would you like to be? Why?
5. Who do you fit in with? Why?
6. Who do you not fit in with? Why?
7. What are you thankful for?
8. What do you want that you do not have? Do you want what someone else has? If so, why?
9. What do you need that you do not have?
10. When would you like to get what you want and need?
11. What can you become?
12. Where would you like to live?
13. What excites you, motivates you, and gets your energy flowing?
14. What would you do each day if you could? List everything.
15. What motivates you?
16. What success do you feel you deserve to have in your life?
17. What have you succeeded at? Personally? Professionally? Socially? Financially? Charitably? Mentally? Physically?

18. What rating would you give each area of your life at this time? From 1 to 10?

19. What one word best describes your life? Excellent? Great? Struggle?

20. What feeling would success give you? Why?

21. What are you curious about?

22. What do you do to make your living? If you are not working why not?

23. What do you like and dislike about your current/last job?

24. What made you choose your current/last job?

25. What do your family and friends think of your current/last job?

26. What is your ultimate way to make your living?

27. What other jobs have you done in the past?

28. What jobs have you ever been fired from? If so, why? Have you ever fired anyone? If so, how did that make you feel?

29. Who do you look up to or model yourself after?

30. Who would you like to meet and why? What would you ask them?

Strengths & Weaknesses

1. List your strengths in all areas of your life.
2. What strengths do you want?
3. List your weaknesses in all areas of your life.
4. Which weaknesses would you like to work on the most?
5. Who makes you feel inferior? If so, why?
6. Do you doubt your abilities? If so, why?

7. Do you get defensive about certain topics of discussion or questions? List them.
8. Is anyone able to push your buttons? If yes, why?
9. Do you push other people's buttons? If yes, whose and why?

Thinking

1. What do you think about when you first wake up?
2. What do you think about throughout your day?
3. What do you think about before you go to sleep?
4. Do your thoughts help you or hurt you in being more successful?
5. What thoughts do you need to change?

Physical Health

1. How would you rate your physical condition?
2. What kind of exercise do you do and how often?
3. What kind of exercise would you like to do?
4. Do you feel you need to exercise more? If so, what prevents you from exercising more?
5. Do you eat a healthy diet? If not, why not?
6. What kind of eating habits would you like to have?

Mental Health

1. How is your mental health?
2. Is it as strong as you want/need it to be?
3. What mental roadblocks are stopping you from success?

4. List experiences that impacted your mental health.

Financial Health

1. What kind of financial health are you in?
2. Do you spend more than you earn? If so, why?
3. Do you like to buy the latest gadgets, clothes, cars, etc.?
4. Do you have money to invest? If so, what percentage of your weekly earnings?
5. Have you lost money investing? If so, did you allow someone else to make the decisions?
6. Do you own your own business?
7. Have you ever had a business fail? If so, what caused the failure?
8. Do you feel you will be able to retire?
9. Does your financial situation allow you to live the life you want? Why or why not?

Sleep

1. How many hours of sleep do you get each night?
2. Do you use an alarm to wake you each day?
3. If you use an alarm do you hit the snooze button or do you get up immediately?

Decisions

1. Do you feel in control of all areas of your life? If not, who is in control of these areas?

2. What decisions did you make in the past that you wish you had not made?
3. What decisions did you not make that you wish you had?
4. What opportunities did you miss out on because of your decisions or lack of decisions?
5. What decisions did you let others make for you that you wish you had not?
6. What decisions are you still letting others make for you?
7. What decisions are you making that push you closer to or further away from success?
8. What kind of decisions would you like to be able to make?
9. Do you give in to group choices even if you disagree?
10. Do you blame others for where you are in life?
11. Are you good at making quick decisions?
12. Do you avoid/ignore problems hoping they will simply go away?
13. What would you like to do that you have not?
14. What has been holding you back?

Likes/Dislikes

1. What is your favorite food? Why?
2. What food do you dislike? Why?
3. What is your favorite color? Why?
4. What colors do you dislike? Why?
5. What is your favorite movie or type of movie? Why?
6. What is your least favorite movie or type of movie? Why?

7. What is your favorite music or type of music? Why?
8. What music do you dislike? Why?
9. What is your favorite book or poem? Why?
10. What is your least favorite book or poem? Why?
11. Who is your favorite person? Why?
12. Who is your least favorite person? Why?
13. What are your favorite things to do? Why?
14. What are your least favorite things to do? Why?
15. Do you like people who are different than you (religion, race, culture, sex, etc.)? Why or why not? Is it based on true experiences or on what you hear, read, see, but have not experienced?
16. List any other likes or dislikes you have. Also list why you like or dislike something.
17. What areas of your life do you like?
18. What areas of your life do you dislike?
19. What are you doing to change those areas?
20. Is anyone helping you achieve your dreams/goals?
21. Do you feel alive and feel that you are making progress, or do you feel stuck?
22. Do you go to sleep anticipating the next day or regretting what may come your way?
23. Do you wake up feeling energized and ready to get started or do you roll over and go back to sleep, wishing it was not time to face the day?
24. Are you ready to live life to the fullest?

25. Do you want the rest of your life to be different than the previous part of your life?

Personality

1. Do you have a sense of humor?
2. Do others think you have a sense of humor?
3. Are you a fun person to be around?
4. How do you respond to pressure?
5. Do you like to lead or follow?
6. Do you trust others to do their job/part or would you rather do everything yourself?
7. When do you have a positive attitude?
8. When do you have a negative attitude?
9. What makes you angry and why?
10. What would you like to change about your personality?

Beliefs

1. What are you current beliefs about achieving your dreams/goals?
2. What beliefs prevent you from achieving your dreams?
3. What beliefs do you need to reach your potential?
4. Are you a confident person? Why or why not?
5. In what areas are you confident?
6. In what areas do you lack confidence?
7. Are you confident about trying new things?

8. Do you feel confident around certain people and then lose your confidence around others? Who and why?
9. Do you respect yourself? Why or why not?
10. Do you think you are smart?
11. Do good things happen to you in your life? Give examples.
12. Do bad things happen to you in your life? Give examples.
13. Do you believe good things will happen to you? If so, why?
14. Do you believe bad things will happen to you? If so, why?
15. What are your beliefs about sex, race, politics, immigration, etc.?
16. Are you religious/spiritual? If so, why?
17. Do you know anyone who always sees the negative side of things?
18. Do you know anyone who always sees the positive side of things?
19. Where do you fall in between those two?
20. What is your definition of happiness?
21. What will make you happy in all areas of your life?
22. Do you feel you deserve to be happy and successful? Why or why not?

Values

1. List your values?
2. List the values you have broken at some point in your life?
3. List the values you wish you had, but for some reason cannot hold up to?
4. How would you tell others to live their life if they asked you?

5. What can you do right now to start turning your life in the direction you want?
6. Do you have integrity?
7. Do you have character?
8. Do you do the right things?

Emotions

1. List the emotions you feel throughout any given day?
2. What emotions are missing?
3. Which emotions would you like to get rid of?
4. What makes you feel good?
5. What makes you feel bad?
6. Are you ever depressed? If so, what percentage of the time?

Comfort Zone

1. Do you like to try new things? Why or why not?
2. Do you like to take risks? Why or why not?
3. Describe your feelings when you do try new things/take risks?
4. What would you like to do that you fear doing?
5. Do you always have to do things perfectly? If so, why?
6. Do you wait before you try new things to make sure you are 100% ready?
7. Do you know who and what situations make you feel uncomfortable?

8. Do you have things that cause you mental or physical pain? Such as no money, no family, no friends, no social life, no career, poor health.
9. What scares you the most? Is it real or made up in your mind?
10. Do you get stressed out? If so, what causes it?

Failure/Criticism/Rejection

1. What have you failed at?
2. Do you know the reasons for your failure?
3. How did you feel when you failed?
4. Do you think you will always fail?
5. How do you respond to personal and professional criticism?
6. How do you respond to personal and professional rejection?
7. Do you know the reasons for your criticism/rejection?
8. Do you worry about what others will say?
9. Do you judge yourself harshly?
10. How long did it take you to bounce back from failure/criticism/rejection?
11. How do you react under pressure or when things do not go exactly as planned?
12. Will you keep going when success does not come instantly and your initial excitement wears off?
13. How do you plan for failure/criticism/rejection? Are you always ready?

14. How do you choose to look at the problems/roadblocks you encounter?
15. When things go wrong, do you seek solutions immediately or do you get down on yourself? How long is it before you start to correct the problem?

Greatness

1. How does your life impact other people, animals, nature, etc.? List the good and bad.
2. Is the world a better place because you are here?
3. How can you make it better?
4. Do you feel you are living a meaningful life? What is your purpose? Do you have one?
5. What would you like your purpose to be?

Commitment

1. Do you do what you say you are going to do? Why or why not?
2. List the times you did not do what you said you were going to do.
3. Did you let other people down by not doing what you said you were going to do?
4. How do you feel when you accomplish what you said?
5. How do you feel when you do not accomplish what you said?
6. What are you willing to commit to in your life?
7. Are you willing to be scrutinized and criticized for your dreams/goals?

8. Are you willing to embarrass yourself in order to fulfill your dreams/goals?

Competition/Uniqueness

1. Do you like competing with others? Why or why not?
2. In what areas of your life do you like to compete? Why?
3. In what areas of your life do you not like to compete? Why not?
4. What gives you a competitive edge? It separates you from others.
5. What gives others an edge over you?
6. How can you best use your qualities, strengths, and uniqueness to your advantage?

Focus

1. In what areas of your life do you have trouble focusing?
2. In what areas of your life can you maintain focus?
3. Why can you focus at certain times and not at other times?
4. What kind of disruptions do you experience during your day?
5. Do you focus on what you want in your life?
6. Do you focus on what you do not want in your life?
7. Do you focus on what others have and you do not?

Excuses

1. Do you ever make up excuses for not accomplishing something?
2. In what areas of your life do you use excuses and why?

www.ingramcontent.com/pod-product-compliance
Lightning Source LLC
Chambersburg PA
CBHW071705040426
42446CB00011B/1922